MIRACLES &
MOMENTS
of GRACE

ALSO BY NANCY B. KENNEDY

Make It, Shake It, Mix It Up
Even the Sound Waves Obey Him

MIRACLES &
MOMENTS
of GRACE

INSPIRING STORIES FROM
MILITARY CHAPLAINS

BY NANCY B. KENNEDY

LEAFWOOD
PUBLISHERS

MIRACLES & MOMENTS OF GRACE
INSPIRING STORIES FROM MILITARY CHAPLAINS

LEAFWOOD
P U B L I S H E R S

Copyright 2011 by Nancy B. Kennedy

ISBN 978-0-89112-269-2
LCCN 2010046193

Printed in the United States of America

Scripture quotations, unless otherwise noted, are from The Holy Bible, New
International Version. Copyright 1984, International Bible Society. Used by permission of
Zondervan Publishers.

LIBRARY OF CONGRESS CATALOGING-IN-PUBLICATION DATA
Miracles and moments of grace: inspiring stories from military chaplains / by Nancy B.
Kennedy.
  p. cm.
  Includes bibliographical references and index.
  ISBN 978-0-89112-269-2
  1. Military chaplains--United States--Biography. I. Kennedy, Nancy B.
  UH23.M56 2011
  355.3'47092273--dc22

                                                                    2010046193

Cover and Interior text design by Thinkpen Design, Inc.

Published in association with William K. Jensen Literary Agency,
119 Bampton Court, Eugene, Oregon 97404

Leafwood Publishers
1626 Campus Court
Abilene, Texas 79601
1-877-816-4455 toll free

For current information about all Leafwood titles, visit our Web site:
www.leafwoodpublishers.com

              10 11 12 13 14 15 / 7 6 5 4 3 2 1

For all my chaplains,

and for every chaplain

whose story should be told

Table of Contents

Introduction. 11

1. Don't Go in There! 20
   CHAPLAIN JAMES BLOUNT, MAJOR, U.S. ARMY

2. You Might As Well Pray 27
   CHAPLAIN DOUGLAS WAITE, CAPTAIN, U.S. NAVY

3. The Last Letter. 30
   CHAPLAIN JOANNE MARTINDALE, LIEUTENANT COLONEL, NEW JERSEY ARMY
      NATIONAL GUARD

4. I Need Prayers!. 36
   CHAPLAIN THOMAS GILLS, MAJOR, U.S. AIR FORCE

5. The Christmas Card 39
   CHAPLAIN MICHAEL WHITE, MAJOR, ALABAMA ARMY NATIONAL GUARD

6. A Visit from Lieutenant Dan 43
   CHAPLAIN STEVEN SATTERFIELD, CAPTAIN, COLORADO ARMY NATIONAL GUARD
   CORPORAL WILLIAM SEO, MEDIC, U.S. ARMY

7. The Whispered Service 48
   CHAPLAIN HENRY LAMAR HUNT, COLONEL, U.S. ARMY, RETIRED

8. The Loss of So Many 52
   CHAPLAIN GEORGE PUCCIARELLI, CAPTAIN, U.S. NAVY, RETIRED
   CHAPLAIN ARNOLD RESNICOFF, CAPTAIN, U.S. NAVY, RETIRED
   CHAPLAIN DANNY WHEELER, COMMANDER, U.S. NAVY RESERVE, RETIRED

9. Surrounded by Sharks 61
   CHAPLAIN WALTER BEAN, LIEUTENANT COLONEL, U.S. AIR FORCE

10. Jesus Loves You!. 65
    CHAPLAIN GREGG HAZLETT, LIEUTENANT, U.S. NAVY

11. Tracked Down 68
    CHAPLAIN CHRISTOPHER REEDER, CAPTAIN, U.S. AIR FORCE

12. Give Me Jesus. 73
    CHAPLAIN STEVEN SCHAICK, COLONEL, U.S. AIR FORCE

13. The Hand of God 77
Chaplain Timothy Bohr, Major, U.S. Army Reserve

14. Did I Really Cuss? 82
Chaplain Billy Baugham, Major, U.S. Army, Retired

15. Ping Pong Buddies 87
Chaplain Chad Bellamy, Captain, U.S. Air Force

16. A Sorrowful Sacrifice 92
Chaplain Eddie Barnett, Lieutenant Colonel, U.S. Army

17. A Fateful Fireguard 95
Chaplain Joseph Lawhorn, Captain, U.S. Army
Chaplain John Routzahn, Lieutenant Colonel, U.S. Army

18. A Song of Prayer 99
Chaplain Lorraine Potter, Major General, U.S. Air Force, Retired

19. Looking into Hell 102
Chaplain Laurence Bazer, Lieutenant Colonel, Massachusetts Army
    National Guard
Chaplain Brad Hoffman, Commander, U.S. Navy Reserve

20. A Single Death.. 108
Chaplain Stan Giles, Lieutenant Colonel, Tennessee Air National Guard

21. I'm Not Going Back There 113
Chaplain John Groth, Lieutenant Colonel, U.S. Air Force Reserve, Retired

22. Thank You, Mercy! 117
Chaplain John Owen, Commander, U.S. Navy

23. I'll Do Anything.. 122
Chaplain Beverly Barnett, Lieutenant Colonel, U.S. Air Force, Retired

24. A Chaplain's Cross 126
Chaplain Dallas Little, Captain, U.S. Air Force

25. A Mother's Photo 130
Chaplain Richard Martin, Colonel, U.S. Army, Retired

26. Searching for Scott 134
Chaplain David Alexander, Lieutenant, U.S. Navy (Marines)

27. Tining for Home 140
Chaplain Brad Lewis, Captain, U.S. Army

28. Sailor on the Run... 143
Chaplain Dudley Johnson, Commander, U.S. Navy, Retired

29. The Rockets' Red Glare.................................... 147
CHAPLAIN JASON HESSELING, MAJOR, U.S. ARMY

30. A Marine's Prayer 151
CHAPLAIN DEBORAH LUETHJE MARIYA, LIEUTENANT COMMANDER, U.S. NAVY, RETIRED

31. My Soul Is Safe 154
CHAPLAIN WAYNE GARCIA, MAJOR, U.S. ARMY

32. Easter in Fallujah.. 159
CHAPLAIN JOHN MORRIS, MAJOR, MINNESOTA ARMY NATIONAL GUARD

33. These Sacred Moments 163
CHAPLAIN JASON PETERS, MAJOR, U.S. AIR FORCE

34. A Young Chaplain's Decision............................ 167
CHAPLAIN EV SCHRUM, COLONEL, U.S. AIR FORCE, RETIRED

35. Dieu Vous Aime... 170
CHAPLAIN HAROLD CARLSON, COLONEL, U.S. ARMY, RETIRED

36. Out of the Ashes 173
CHAPLAIN BARBARA SHERER, COLONEL, U.S. ARMY

37. A Person of Life... 176
CHAPLAIN WILLIAM "DAVE" LOGAN, CAPTAIN, U.S. AIR FORCE

38. A Jungle Retreat... 179
CHAPLAIN RICHARD ROJAS, CAPTAIN, U.S. AIR FORCE

39. Start Off with a Prayer 186
CHAPLAIN JACK STANLEY, MAJOR, U.S. AIR FORCE

40. The Gift of Life 191
CHAPLAIN DENNIS ALESON, LIEUTENANT COLONEL, U.S. AIR FORCE, RETIRED

41. A Whole New Life....................................... 196
CHAPLAIN RICHARD "MIKE" WARNER, LIEUTENANT COLONEL, U.S. AIR FORCE

42. A Baptism at Sea 201
CHAPLAIN JASON ROCHESTER, LIEUTENANT, U.S. NAVY (COAST GUARD)

43. Golfing in a Combat Zone 204
CHAPLAIN DAVID SIFFERD, MAJOR, U.S. ARMY RESERVE

44. Immoderate Rains....................................... 209
CHAPLAIN JOSH WHITE, CAPTAIN, SOUTH CAROLINA ARMY NATIONAL GUARD

45. Pull Your Reserve!....................................... 214
CHAPLAIN ROBERT SAUNDERS, COLONEL, U.S. ARMY, RETIRED

46. Where's Our Ice Cream?................................. 217
CHAPLAIN GLYGER BEACH, COLONEL, U.S. ARMY RESERVE, RETIRED

47. Laying Down Our Sorrows 220
CHAPLAIN JAMES PENNINGTON, CAPTAIN, U.S. ARMY

48. I'm Doing Fine... 223
CHAPLAIN BARRY WHITE, LIEUTENANT COLONEL, U.S. ARMY, RETIRED

49. On the Maine Line 225
CHAPLAIN SHERI SNIVELY, COMMANDER, U.S. NAVY RESERVE

50. The Presence of Christ in a War Zone 228
CHAPLAIN GORDON TERPSTRA, LIEUTENANT COLONEL, U.S. ARMY RESERVE

Acknowledgements.................................... 233

Endnotes... 235

Index 236

Introduction

"Ma'am, thanks for contacting me. I'm sitting here in my hooch in Bagh-dad. It is nice to know someone wants to tell our stories."

These words of gratitude came to me from an Air Force chaplain deployed in Iraq last year. He had gotten word that I was writing a book of stories told by military chaplains, and he had a story to tell me.

How I came to write this book is a story in itself—a story of ordinary circumstances turned extraordinary through divinely appointed chance.

Last fall, my husband, John, and I were enjoying the company of Air Force Chaplain Lieutenant Colonel Gary Ziccardi and his wife, Rosalind, an ordained Presbyterian minister. I hadn't seen Gary since we spent the summers of our teen years at a church camp in upstate New York. Neither John nor I had ever met Rosalind, although I had talked with her several times on the phone, and we had exchanged Christmas cards down through the years.

After several hours of catching up on our lives, Gary said he wanted to tell me a story. It concerned a care package we had mailed to him during his deployment in Southwest Asia, one of two separations he has endured from Rosalind and their two sons over the years. He was slated to be chaplain for a military police force over Christmas that year, so I had resolved to make sure I remembered both of them during the holidays.

In the days following Thanksgiving, I assembled a care package for Gary. I started with a plastic desktop Christmas tree adorned with tiny ornaments and lights. I'm not usually enamored of plastic anything, but I had fond memories of a small tree my parents sent to me one year to decorate my college dorm room. Rosalind had mentioned several kinds of candy Gary particularly liked, so I shopped the bulk bins at the grocery store for big bags of sweets.

Our adult Sunday class at church had recently compiled a package for soldiers that one of our members, a military recruiter, was able to put on a plane departing from McGuire Air Force Base. He had suggested including muffin or cake mixes. For the class's box, I was thrilled to find muffin mixes called American Apple Pie muffins. They were just the thing! In Gary's box, I included some brownie mixes, since Rosalind had said that he liked chocolate.

Of course, Gary sent me an e-mail note thanking me for the box. It had arrived a few weeks before Christmas. He was tickled to have a Christmas tree, the only one on the base. And he mentioned setting the candy out on his desk for people to enjoy as they passed by.

Over dinner that night at our home, however, Gary wanted to tell us what happened to the brownie mixes. Not having the ingredients or means for making the brownies, he approached the military police kitchen staff, who said they'd see what they could do.

Meanwhile, Gary began preparing a Christmas Eve service for the soldiers. Upon his arrival in September, the military police had graciously allowed Gary to use their small break room for his Sunday services and a weekday Bible study. They were happy to let him use the room for the Christmas Eve service, which he scheduled for 9:30

in the evening. He began praying for a quiet and peaceful service. The correctional facility could become quite rowdy at times, and Gary feared that disruptions could mar the holy atmosphere he desired for remembering Christ's birth.

In the days leading up to the service, he was thrilled to receive another package in the mail, one from Rosalind that contained small wrapped gifts she thought he might want to pass out—small picture frames, snacks, mini pots of flowering seeds, decks of cards, inflatable and soft squeeze balls, personal toiletries, and other items. He also got word that the kitchen had gotten the ingredients needed for the brownies, and they could be made up for a party following the service.

Preparing to start the service that Christmas Eve, Gary glanced around the chapel. Normally, Gary said, two or three soldiers might come to his Sunday services. Because of the enduring nature of Christmas traditions, he expected a few more at the Christmas Eve service. Still, he was astonished to find the seats filling up. It became a standing-room-only affair! He was grateful for all who had come to hear once again the Christmas story of God's boundless love for mankind.

During the service, just as Gary had prayed, peace and calm reigned. The assembled soldiers sang Christmas carols to Gary's guitar accompaniment in a reverent atmosphere, and not a single commotion interrupted Gary's homily. After the service ended, Gary gestured to a table that had been set up with the gifts and food and invited everyone to enjoy both. These gifts were sent from home out of love for them, Gary said, just as God had sent his Son out of love.

At the service, Gary had counted 27 personnel in attendance in addition to himself—28 in all. Upon being invited to the table, every person picked out a gift and enjoyed a brownie. After everyone had gone through the line, Gary was astonished to find that the gifts and brownies laid out on the table were exactly enough to go around. Exactly enough!

For me, the story was a powerful example of God's grace in the lives of military personnel and the family and friends who support them. I shudder when I think of how infrequently I get my act together sufficiently to show others that I am thinking of them. Although God can accomplish everyday miracles like this one without our help, I am grateful to have played a part in this incredible story.

As for Gary? Something he said that night started the wheels in motion for this book. After telling his story, he paused and said, "You know, we chaplains have *hundreds* of these stories!" I thought, *Hmmm. Hundreds of stories!* Rosalind, a writer herself, urged me to consider writing a book of these stories. I needed no further encouragement.

Once I began soliciting stories, I was besieged with responses. My chaplains stacked up like jets on a runway, eager to share their stories, thrilled that someone wanted to tell them. Over and over, I heard words of gratitude—like those of the deployed Air Force chaplain in his quarters in Baghdad—from these hardworking and self-sacrificing spiritual advisors and mentors.

The chaplains in this book carry on an honorable and respected tradition of service to our country. The U.S. military has had chaplains almost from its inception. The official start of the military chaplaincy is widely considered to be July 29, 1775. On this day, Congress recognized chaplains in the national army with a standing equal to that of captain and a monthly pay of twenty dollars.[1]

Perhaps it was the actions of early chaplains that persuaded Congress to recognize their service in this way. Three months earlier, one Revolutionary War chaplain had impressed General George Washington with his selfless and tireless devotion to the troops. David Avery, a pastor from Vermont, was seemingly "superior to the weakness of common mortals."[2] After the Battle of Lexington and Concord on April 18, 1775, Avery served as captain of a group of his parishioners, bringing them down to Cambridge, Massachusetts. There, they were assigned to a regiment and Rev. Avery became a full-time chaplain. Two months later, he saw combat at the Battle of Bunker Hill. For his service, Chaplain Avery was lauded as

> Intrepid and fearless in battle, Unwearied in his attentions
> to the sick and wounded—not only nursing them with
> care, but as faithful to their souls as if they were of his
> own parish—with a love for his country so strong that it
> became a passion—cheerful under privations, and ready
> for any hardship—never losing in the turmoil of camp that
> warmth and glowing piety which characterizes the devoted
> minister of God.[3]

A few years later, on June 23, 1780, at the Battle of Springfield, N.J., Chaplain James Caldwell made history for his patriotism and quick thinking. Rev. Caldwell, a Presbyterian minister from Elizabethtown, discovered that in the midst of battle, Patriot troops had run out of wadding and could no longer fire their muskets. He rushed into a nearby church and gathered up its hymnbooks. Returning to the battlefield, he began handing out the hymnals so that soldiers could use their pages as wadding. So many well-known hymns of the day were written by Isaac Watts that as the soldiers loaded their muskets, Chaplain Caldwell cried out, "Give them Watts, boys, give them Watts!"[4]

Chaplains continued serving our country, their courage and selflessness noted time and again. When I began writing this book and asked chaplains to tell me their stories, many of them first asked whether I had heard the most famous story of the military chaplaincy—the tale known to most people simply as the story of The Four Chaplains.

During World War II, on the night of February 3, 1943, the troop ship the USAT *Dorchester* was torpedoed by a German submarine off the coast of Newfoundland. With the electrical system knocked out, the ship was instantly plunged into total darkness. Men panicked and chaos ensued as they tried to grope their way out from below collapsed decks to evacuate the listing ship.

Aboard the ship were four U.S. Army chaplains—Jewish Rabbi Alexander Goode, Catholic priest Father John Washington and two Protestant chaplains, Methodist minister George Fox and the Rev. Clark Poling of the Reformed Church in America. The chaplains, all four of them lieutenants, worked to calm the men, tend to the wounded and help them into lifeboats.

But it quickly became apparent that there weren't enough lifeboats, nor enough life jackets, for the 902 servicemen, merchant seamen and civilians on board. As the supply of life jackets ran out, the four chaplains took off their jackets and handed them to men in need.

One survivor, John Ladd, was stunned when he saw one of the chaplains remove his life jacket. It was "the finest thing I have seen or hope to see this side of heaven," he said.[5]

Bracing themselves on the tilting deck, the four chaplains linked arms and began to pray—in a melange of English, Latin and Hebrew—and sing hymns of faith. Another survivor, Private William B. Bednar, recalls floating in the icy, oil-smeared water amid debris and dead bodies and hearing men all around him praying, crying, pleading for rescue. He adds, "I could also hear the chaplains preaching courage. Their voices were the only thing that kept me going."[6]

Survivor Grady Clark later shared his last sight of them:

> As I swam away from the ship, I looked back. The flares had lighted everything. The bow came up high and she slid under. The last thing I saw, the four chaplains were up there praying for the safety of the men. They had done everything they could. I did not see them again. They themselves did not have a chance without their life jackets.[7]

As the ship went under, many survivors recall hearing the chaplains as they recited in unison the bracing words of The Lord's Prayer— "Our Father, who art in Heaven, hallowed be Thy name. Thy kingdom come, thy will be done, on earth as it is in Heaven. . . ." With these words, the four chaplains joined the 672 men who died at sea that night.

Incredible as the inspiring story of The Four Chaplains is, it's an entirely true story. Likewise, in this book, you are reading stories that are absolutely true. I have at times changed the names of people mentioned, to protect their privacy and the confidentiality of their stories, but nothing about the stories themselves is fictional. Some of the chaplains told their own stories, having written articles, books, blogs or personal journals, while I interviewed other chaplains and told their stories in their own words.

It is my privilege here, then, to tell the stories of these dedicated men and women entrusted with the spiritual well-being of our country's armed forces. God bless them, and through them, you.

NANCY B. KENNEDY

MARCH 2011

Some want to live
within the sound
of church or chapel bell;
I want to run a rescue shop
within a yard of hell.

—C. T. Studd

1

DON'T GO IN THERE!

CHAPLAIN JAMES BLOUNT

MAJOR, U.S. ARMY

Valor is a gift. Those having it never know for sure
whether they have it till the test comes.

CARL SANDBURG

The morning of November 4, 2002, I woke up in my pod in Kosovo. I was coming to the end of a six-month tour attached to the 1st Infantry Division that had been deployed with the Multinational Brigade East peace support operation.

Getting out of bed, I prepared to do physical training (PT) outside on my own. The morning was chilly—cold really—so I dressed in my full PT outfit: long pants, long sleeves, jacket and cap. I had barely made it out the door when I heard a commotion and saw a soldier running toward me. He was agitated and shouting. He got up so close to me he was practically bumping me, and screaming so loudly he was almost incoherent. It took me a second, but then I understood him.

"Chaplain! Chaplain!" he shouted. "There's a guy firing a weapon in the room!"

I looked up and saw soldiers streaming out of their barracks, running in all directions. Everyone was yelling: "He's firing!" "He's shooting through the walls!"

Without even thinking, I started off in the direction of the shots. As I walked, a soldier running past me yelled, "Don't go in there!" All around me, I heard soldiers saying the same thing. Behind me, a voice having some authority warned me not to go any closer—a senior ranking officer, I guessed—but I didn't turn around to look.

I couldn't tell you why I didn't stop. I just kept walking at an even pace until I got to the steps of the barracks. The firing had stopped by now, although it was still pandemonium all around. Even so, I could hear a voice from inside the building.

"You'd better not come in here," the voice warned. Two times, I heard it. It was the soldier with the gun.

What did I do? After a second or two, I started up the steps. Like before, I didn't hesitate. I had no feeling of fear. To this day, I can't explain why I didn't turn around. I wasn't thinking; I was only reacting. I wasn't in control of my actions right then. I believe God was.

When I walked through the door, I saw the soldier standing in front of me, some ways into the building. I didn't know him. He was a new guy. He was in full combat gear: flak jacket, helmet, body armor. He looked like he was going into combat. He was fully armed with rounds.

And he was aiming his M16 rifle straight at me.

The soldier began walking, quickly, toward me. He flicked the safety off. That's when the fear hit. I was terrified. I had done a tour in Iraq, but as a chaplain I'd never been directly targeted.

As the soldier got closer to me, I detected a change in his face, the tiniest bit of softening. He probably saw the terror in my face, and knew I was the chaplain. I was one of the oldest people in the unit, so I was pretty recognizable. I'd been in the civilian world a long time. My calling card was a duffel bag full of candy that I liked to share with people. He probably realized I wasn't a threat!

Even so, he kept coming at me, weapon aimed, finger on the trigger. Within milliseconds, he was right in front of me, the rifle only a foot from my chest. We stared at each other. Later, it struck me that I stood there with my arms straight at my sides—I didn't even know enough to put my hands up in surrender. We didn't say anything for the longest time. Then the soldier spoke.

"I told you not to come in here," he said. Though his face had softened, he still had a hard, hard look in his eyes.

"I know," I answered him. "But I came in here to talk to you."

And talk, we did. This soldier was deeply troubled—he had left the Marines recently and had come back into the Army. He may have been forced out of the Marines. He felt like he hadn't been treated well by his fellow soldiers, that they had been giving him a hard time because he had come from the Marines. He felt like a failure. And he let it all come spilling out.

For about an hour, we stood right where we were. As he vented, the soldier never lowered his gun. It was pointed at me the whole time. Finally, we moved further into the room. I don't remember who suggested it. I sat down on a bunk, and he sat on a chair, the gun across his lap.

While we talked, it was clear to me that the soldier was suicidal. I believe he wanted to end his life, to put an end to the pain. Either he wanted to kill himself, or he wanted to force someone to kill him. Firing his weapon into the walls was his way of getting the other guys out of the barracks. But everyone had left their weapons and ammunition behind. This guy was fully loaded. He could take a lot of guys down with him. He could take me down with him.

Hours went by. The whole time we talked, we were aware of movement outside. I never saw anyone clearly, even though the back door of the barracks was open. Through the door, we saw fast-moving shadows. I thought maybe a unit had been brought in, but I couldn't tell for sure. Eventually, we heard people running on top of the building. It was a prefab metal structure, so we could hear it clearly. We both knew we were surrounded.

Although he kept talking, I sensed that the soldier still wanted someone to take the decision of life or death out of his hands. At one point, he decided he was going to go out and engage the soldiers, that he was basically going to commit suicide and take out as many people as he could. I said to him, "If you go out, I'm going to walk out there with you." I think he began to see how much I cared about him. He backed down.

Still, he remained in combat mode, looking around stealthily, ready to make a move. He got up periodically, checking the sides of the building, making precise moves. His combat training was obvious.

Periodically, we heard voices outside repeating the same sentence over and over again. "He needs to come out with no weapons! He needs to come out with no weapons!" Although we didn't know it then, word had come down that time was running out, that the stand-off had gone on long enough. The guys outside were getting edgy. They were preparing to strike.

While the soldier talked, I listened. But I also had a frantic conversation going on in my head: *How am I going to talk this guy down? Should I tackle him? Should I take his weapon?* I hadn't had any training in negotiating at all. None whatsoever.

In the end, I didn't make a move of any sort. I believe the Lord kept me from escalating the danger of the situation. The soldier talked on and on. After about five hours, he seemed to run out of steam. He turned his focus on me, not in anger but in a kind of sympathy.

"You look terrible, Chaplain. You're afraid! Look, you're shaking," he said. "You're tired of being in here, aren't you?" And, incredibly, he started to laugh.

It was then that I realized the soldier probably wasn't going to kill me. I suggested to him that it might be a good time for us to pray. "Yes, I want to pray," the soldier said.

I believe now that prayer broke the crisis. I've never had anything bad come from prayer! I prayed, then he prayed, then I prayed some more. It sounded to me like he had some background of faith. After we finished, I suggested that we leave the building. He started to agree when he stopped himself.

"Wait!" the soldier said. "I'm hungry."

With that, he reached into his jacket and pulled out a chocolate muffin. He was getting ready to take a bite, but he paused and looked over at me. He broke the muffin apart and handed half to me. "Here," he said. "You have a piece."

I don't know what it was about the muffin, but at that moment I resolved that I was going to get this soldier out of there alive. I made up my mind then that nobody was going to shoot anybody.

"Let's just walk out of here," I said again. Then I asked if I could say one more prayer.

After I had finished, he stood up, leaving his weapon on the chair. He said, "Come here, Chaplain," and he patted me on the shoulder. He took off all his combat gear, all his rounds, and gave everything to me. Finally, he handed over his gun.

"Buddy," he said. "I'm tired, too. Are you ready to go?"

"Yes," I said. "I'm ready to go."

It was just 200 yards to the medical clinic, down a dirt road, so I suggested that was where we should head. I offered to go out first and he agreed. As we emerged from the building, we had the sense of people moving away from the building. As before, we could see only moving shadows.

But then the soldier said to me, "Look to the right, Chaplain. Look to the left." I did. All around us snipers were in position. They were everywhere. There were still at the ready.

The medical people came out of the clinic and started walking toward us. I sensed people following behind us, one person so close I probably could have touched him with a finger. Without even looking behind me, I handed back the soldier's gear and his weapon and ammo.

The crisis was over. The medical director escorted the soldier into the clinic and I was released into the care of my brigade chaplain. "We need to talk," he said.

On July 14, 2004, I received the Soldier's Medal for my actions of that day. I was honored for risking my own life to save the lives of others from a homicidal soldier, for displaying personal bravery and peacefully resolving a potentially tragic situation. After the incident, a commander from another unit said, "Chaplain, you're done. You don't have to do another thing for your country. You have made your contribution. Just be happy and enjoy your life."

But, do you know what? I don't feel like a hero. In fact, after the incident, I spent hours with my brigade chaplain and another chaplain crying like a baby. I felt an overwhelming sense of my own failings—failings toward my wife and my kids, sinfulness in my own personal life. I felt a deep conviction that I needed to repent and ask forgiveness. The chaplains put their arms around me while I grieved, and they prayed with me.

I later heard that the soldier was getting the help he needed. And I believe in my heart that today he is doing fine. Looking back, though, I believe God allowed me to walk into this situation not just for the sake of that soldier, but for myself as well. After that incident, I felt closer to God than I ever have in my entire life. The real hero that day was God.

Chaplain James W. Blount is a Southern Baptist Army chaplain assigned through the North American Mission Board. He has worked with the Foreign Mission Board in Conakry, Guinea, and served as a pastor. He was deployed to Iraq in 2004. He and his wife, Marsha, have four grown children and one grandson, Cameron.

2

You Might As Well Pray

Chaplain Douglas Waite

Captain, U.S. Navy

In the late 1980s, I was stationed at the U.S. Naval hospital in Yokosuka, Japan. I was a young lieutenant on my second tour as a chaplain and the only chaplain assigned to the hospital.

There was a high-ranking captain at the hospital, a doctor who was undoubtedly the best surgeon there. He was the doctor you'd want to operate on you if you needed surgery. But the doctor's bedside manner was terrible. He was loud and arrogant and rude; the staff literally trembled when he walked by. Everybody tried to stay out of his way, even me.

One day, after dining off the base, the doctor contracted salmonella poisoning. He came to the hospital in bad shape; he was in a lot of pain. He was so miserable he thought he must be dying. Over the next few days, nothing anybody did at the hospital helped him. Medical science was failing him.

The doctor's pain did nothing to improve his disposition. He was a horrible patient, yelling and screaming and demanding attention. The nurses were all scared of him.

A few days into his illness, I was getting ready to leave the hospital for the day, eager to get home to my wife and kids. But something stopped me. I heard the Lord say clearly to me: *Go down there and pray for the doctor.*

"No way!" I protested. "I am *not* going down there!"

But, of course, I couldn't ignore the voice of the Lord. I went down to the doctor's floor. When I got there, the nurses implored me not to go into his room. "He'll take your head off!" they warned.

It was a distinct possibility. The doctor was way above me in rank, an 0-6 captain to my 0-3 lieutenant.

Even so, I appeared in the doorway.

"What do *you* want, Chaplain?" he snarled at me.

"Well, sir," I said. "I came down here to pray for you."

"*What?*" he cried in disbelief.

"That's right," I said. "I came down here to pray for you."

"Well," he huffed. "You're here, so you might as well go ahead. Nothing else has worked."

My prayer was a simple one. "Lord, please touch the doctor and heal him," I prayed. With that, I walked out. I didn't stay around for the doctor's reaction.

The next morning, I arrived at the hospital at about 7:30 a.m. The phone was ringing as I walked into my office. It was the doctor.

"Chaplain," he barked. "I want you down here right now!"

In a panic, I ran down to the doctor's room. I had no idea what I was about to face. When I walked in, the doctor got right to the point.

"Chaplain," he said. "The minute you said that prayer last night, my pain stopped!"

I was astounded! But the doctor wasn't finished.

"I grew up in a Christian family," he continued. "But medical school took me far away from God. This has brought me back."

The doctor went on to make a complete recovery. As a person, he was still gruff and at times overpowering, but his manner softened noticeably. From that day on, he was known to ask every person he treated, "Has the chaplain been over to pray for you yet?" He sure kept me busy, praying for his patients!

The Lord wanted to heal the doctor. I don't know why. I can't tell you how many people I've prayed for who haven't gotten well, even my family and friends. I just know I need to listen to his voice even if I don't want to. When I hear that voice now, I always try to obey it!

Chaplain Douglas Waite has served in the U.S. Navy for 33 years, 27 as a United Methodist chaplain, where he has served with the Marine Corps and the Coast Guard. He was drafted into the Navy during the Vietnam War. Later, he was a pastor in the state of Washington when he felt a call to the military chaplaincy. He has been stationed on three continents and served in Desert Storm and Operation Southern Watch. He was at the Pentagon on 9/11 and later reported to New York City to escort families to Ground Zero. He and his wife, Gail, have five children.

3

THE LAST LETTER

CHAPLAIN JOANNE MARTINDALE
LIEUTENANT COLONEL,
NEW JERSEY ARMY NATIONAL GUARD

I expect to pass through this world but once; any good thing therefore that I

can do, or any kindness that I can show to any fellow creature, let me do it

now; let me not defer or neglect it, for I shall not pass this way again.

ETIENNE DE GRELLET

As a New Jersey National Guardsman, I'm not sure I ever envisioned that on my first night in Iraq I'd be hiking alone in the middle of a pitch-black night to sleeping quarters with no lights and no furniture, and being so tired I'd happily fall into an exhausted sleep on the hard floor.

In January 2005, I was deployed with the 42d Infantry Division to Forward Operating Base (FOB) Speicher outside Tikrit, Iraq. It's a large base, one of the Army's largest, so it was a busy place. I was coming in to relieve another chaplain as divisional support command chaplain and was to have many chaplains under my charge.

The journey from Fort Dix to Tikrit was long and exhausting. We finally came into Iraq from Camp Buehring, Kuwait, on a C-130

Hercules cargo plane, and then boarded a bus to the base. It was a school-bus sized vehicle with about 35 people in it. People were shooting at us as we went along. I was new to combat zones, so I was pretty scared. It wasn't safe anywhere.

We arrived in the middle of the night and reported in for our CHU (Containerized Housing Unit) assignment. As a chaplain, I sort of got pushed to the front of the line. Even so, it was hours before we were assigned our rooms. The sergeant in charge of billeting pointed me in the general direction of my CHU. "It's about a mile and a half down this road," he said.

The sergeant handed me a key, and finished with some dire words. "The key might not work," he said. "If it doesn't, come back and I'll give you another."

The "road" the sergeant pointed me to was gravel-covered, and it was pitch black out. No lights at all. I hate to admit this, but I had forgotten to bring a flashlight. That was a big mistake. I had only moonlight and the stars to guide me along. I started walking. It was hard going; I tripped and fell twice. Finally, I arrived at the CHU with my number on it. The housing units are essentially big white boxes surrounded to the top with sandbags. I tried the key. Of course, it didn't work.

Well, I wasn't about to trek back and get another key. So I looked around for a window. I found one that I was able to reach, so I pushed on it and popped the window out. I dropped my bag in, and then climbed through.

I groped around for a light switch and flipped it on. The lights didn't work. I was alone in the room. Another officer had been assigned to share the room, but she hadn't arrived yet. The room was supposed to have furniture, but it hadn't arrived yet either. That didn't bother me. I just lay down on the floor in my clothes and went to sleep.

I hadn't been asleep more than two hours when there was a knock on the door. "Chaplain, you need to come quickly," a soldier said. "There's been a mass casualty and we need you at the combat hospital."

Now, a mass casualty means 14 or more injured soldiers, so I knew the situation was severe. I leapt up and headed for the door. The current chaplain had been called to the air field on base, which was 15 miles away, so I was the closest chaplain to the combat hospital, just a mile and a half away. My escort drove me to the hospital.

I walked into the hospital, a large room lined on either side with beds. It was a chaotic scene. There had been an IED, an improvised explosive device. Soldiers with head traumas cried out in distress. Hospital carts rolled and crashed into place, as units of blood were rushed to the wounded. Doctors and nurses filled the room, talking and shouting over one another.

My chaplain's uniform has a cross on the lapel and another on the helmet. A surgeon spotted me as soon as I came in. "I'm glad you're here," he said. "There's a soldier who's been asking for a chaplain."

The surgeon led me down the row to a hospital bed. In it lay a soldier who was bleeding out. The doctors had done what they could, but his head wound was too severe. He had only a few minutes to live.

"Please write letters to my family," the dying soldier pleaded with me. I had a notepad in my pocket—something the size of a steno pad—so I took it out. I sat down beside the soldier's bed. "I'm Kevin," the soldier said. "I'm Joanne," I answered.

I leaned in so I could look into Kevin's eyes as I wrote. He took hold of my hand, the hand I was holding the pad with, and wrapped his hand around my fingers. He began to speak. With tears welling in his eyes, he addressed his wife first.

"Dear Beth," he said. "I'm sorry you're not going to see me alive again. Please don't be angry with the Army. It has been an honor to serve my country.

"I'm sorry you're going to have to raise our two children by yourself. But I'll be with you even from heaven. I respect all the decisions you are going to make, and I'll be with you in every one.

"If you decide one day to remarry, I will be there to support you. That will be one lucky man. You've been a wonderful wife, and a wonderful mother. Our children are lucky to have you for a mother."

After a few parting words, Kevin then spoke to his oldest child, a boy about eight years old.

"Son, I am sorry I will not be there to coach your soccer and baseball teams anymore. I will miss that. I enjoyed so much the time we spent together. Don't be angry at the Army. Your dad was serving his country, helping children like you in another land to be free.

"Listen to your mother. She loves you very much. She will tell you stories about us, how thankful I am for you and your sister. I am very proud of you. I know you will grow up to be a fine young man."

Finally, Kevin addressed his daughter, a girl about five years old.

"I'm sorry I won't be able to see you dance again," he said. "I want you to continue with your ballet. You are a beautiful ballerina.

"I'm sorry I won't be there to walk you down the aisle on your wedding day. But know that I will be there anyway. That will be a special man, the one lucky enough to marry you."

When he had finished, Kevin said that he would like us to pray. He wanted to pray first, and so he began.

"Dear Jesus," he prayed. "I'm coming to see you. . . ."

That's as far as he got. Kevin died in my arms in that moment.

I fought back the tears that came into my eyes. I couldn't afford to break down then. I had a lot of soldiers to see before I was through. In fact, even as I lay Kevin's hand down, a soldier in the bed across the aisle called for me. My work at the hospital went on for five hours that night.

When I did finally get back to my room, I cried long and hard. I cried for every soldier I attended to that day, but I cried hardest for Kevin.

Kevin had asked me to send his letters to his family in Georgia. I could have made copies of them, but I sent away the original letters that I wrote there by Kevin's bedside. I left the notes the way they were, blood from his wounds smearing the pages. I wrote a cover note that I attached to the letters to tell Beth the circumstances of her husband's death.

In my cover letter, I offered to visit her, if she would like me to. It's not mandatory for chaplains to visit the family of a fallen soldier, but I felt that I wanted to. "It will be another ten months before I return home," I said. "I'll leave it up to you."

Some time later, I received a letter from Beth saying that she would like me to visit her. And, so, when the time came to return home, I was reunited with my family in Colorado, and then I flew to Georgia to visit Beth. I stayed with Beth and her children for two days. The letters had been very hard for her to read, she told me, but she was grateful that I had attended her husband's last moments on earth.

As a chaplain, I have had twenty-nine people die in my arms. It is a sacred moment—a moment when you remember what this person has meant to so many people. You know that God has put you here for this moment to offer dignity, love and compassion in the face of death. You are a reminder that we are all on earth to honor and cherish each other while we are here. It causes me to recognize God's timing, of things that are beyond my control. I am aware of my fragility, and of the world's great need for healing and compassion amidst all the brokenness. It calls me to bring goodness and love into every encounter of my life.

Chaplain Joanne Martindale is an ordained Presbyterian minister and has served as chaplain at two New Jersey psychiatric hospitals, in addition to her service in the New Jersey Army National Guard. She was called up for service the day of 9/11, to comfort and care for the families of those killed in the Twin Towers. In 2005, she was called up for a tour of duty in Iraq. She is the mother of two sons, Quinn and Ryan.

4

I Need Prayers!

Chaplain Thomas Gills
Major, U.S. Air Force

Almost every crisis you face in the military is an opportunity to grow in faith. Whether it is personal issues or things going on at home that you can't do anything about, or especially when you are facing your own mortality, that's precisely what happens. It causes you to turn to the Lord and seek the help that only he can offer.

In the hospital at Joint Base Balad in Iraq, where I was stationed in 2008, Black Hawk and Chinook helicopters would come in with Marines, soldiers, sailors and airmen wounded in combat. Many of them were in terrible pain, and blood would literally be dripping from their gurneys.

I'd have only a brief moment with the wounded. Walking alongside of them as they were being wheeled in, I'd introduce myself and ask, "Can I pray with you at this moment?"

Most would grab my hand and answer, "Yes, I need prayers, I need prayers, I need prayers!"

Of course, a few would decline to pray. But most were eager to hear that God was in control of their situation. In combat, they had been in control. They had a gun in their hands, they had the power.

But now, wounded, they were utterly helpless, in a position of total surrender.

This is what I would pray:

> *Healing God who knows my pain, Let me feel your Presence right here, right now, And lighten the load my wounds have forced upon me as I fought the evil forces that assaulted me this day. As you knew victory over the scourge of the cross, let me share in that victory now as I bear my sufferings in union with you. Let your healing power enter into every fiber of my being with each cleansing breath, and empower the doctors, nurses, and staff that heal this body as you heal my Spirit. I cast out all fear, doubt, and worry in the name of Jesus, and ask you to fill me with deep peace, for Jesus I trust in you. Jesus I trust in you. Amen.*

I'd only have a minute to pray with them, and then they'd be wheeled into the ER, along with maybe four to eight other patients. In an instant, the beautiful, white, pristine, clean room would suddenly become filled with blood, bright red blood, everywhere.

The next day, I would go back and visit the wounded, after their surgeries, after they'd settled in a bit. So often they would tell me, "I needed God so badly, and it seemed like God spoke to me through you. Then I knew he was real and he would get me through it."

That happened many times. Amazingly, whatever God called to come out of my mouth in prayer in that brief but critical moment would be just exactly what they needed to hear! I received almost the same response from each person.

The wounded face many struggles. One of the most frequent questions I hear is, "Why did God let this happen to me?" My response is always this: "God didn't do this to you, but God will get you through." That's what they need to hear. They already know it, but they need someone to remind them. That's part of my job, helping them turn to God to find the strength they need to endure.

I still get choked up remembering these moments. It has made my own faith stronger. In their dire situations, these soldiers are trusting in God no matter what happens to them, no matter what kind of pain they have to endure. Their ability to turn to God when they're in sorrow or in darkness and not blame him, and not stay in that angry state toward him that some initially are in—to have that experience of going from darkness back to the light of faith—Wow! It makes me deeply grateful for the privilege of ministering to them.

Chaplain Thomas Gills is a Catholic priest from the Archdiocese of Baltimore who has been ordained for 24 years and is serving as an Air Force chaplain for the Archdiocese for the Military Services. Early in his career, Father Gills enlisted in the Navy and later served as an Air Force Reserve chaplain for ten years. He was called to active duty following the 9/11 terrorist attacks and has served in numerous locations, including Germany, Italy, Qatar, United Arab Emirates, Iraq and Afghanistan. This story is adapted and expanded from an interview Father Gills granted to Patricia Coll Freeman of the Catholic Anchor (June 14, 2010).

5

THE CHRISTMAS CARD

CHAPLAIN MICHAEL WHITE

MAJOR, ALABAMA ARMY NATIONAL GUARD

Military families are separated all the time. But it's never as hard as the first time.

In December 1998, I was assigned to South Korea for a year. It was my first unaccompanied tour of duty, as the Army calls it. My wife and children remained in Alabama.

From Alabama to Georgia to Oregon, and then on to Korea, the flight stretched hour-by-hour into 17 long hours. With every passing mile, I thought of how very far from home I was going to be. This was the first time my wife and I had been separated, and this would be our first Christmas apart.

I arrived at the small installation of Camp Sears about a week before Christmas. I was having a tough time emotionally. But I called on the Lord for strength to sustain me. As the unit's chaplain, I wouldn't set a good example if I had difficulty coping in front of the troops.

Christmas Day arrived and I headed to the dining facility for lunch with my new comrades. We had invited a group of young girls from an orphanage in Uijongbu to join us. The oldest girls couldn't have been more than ten years old. The meal we enjoyed with them was almost like home, with plenty of turkey and all the trimmings. It was truly a sumptuous feast.

The children were a delight, too. Our soldiers had bought and wrapped presents for them. A female soldier handed the gifts out. Each girl advanced to accept her gift with a customary display of gratitude. She would approach the presenter with hands outstretched together, palms upward, and bow as the gift was placed in her small hands. As she bowed, every girl said a very polite, "Kamsahamnida!" which means thank you.

After a moment or two, we noticed that the children were not opening their presents. Our interpreter learned that this was another Korean sign of politeness. Recipients of gifts are not supposed to open their gifts in the presence of their givers so as not to embarrass them with an unfavorable reaction. The interpreter urged them to open their gifts right away. Once the children had permission, it didn't take them long to tear off the wrapping paper and gleefully enjoy their gifts. They were things any girl would want to have: dolls, coloring books, toys. I remember one girl was the envy of the other girls when she opened a winter coat.

But of all the gifts that were given and received that Christmas Day—the delicious meal we soldiers enjoyed and the presents that the joyful children opened—there was one that touched my heart more than any of the others.

Earlier that day, the mail clerk had said to me, "Chaplain, I have a piece of mail for you." I was surprised to hear it. I had only been in

Korea ten days, and I didn't know how anyone could have found me. I hadn't received any mail yet. I was excited, but as it was a holiday, I assumed I'd have to wait until the next day to get it, like in the States.

But mail clerks apparently have access to the mail any time they want. As I was sitting down to my meal, he walked by and dropped the envelope onto the table in front of me. Looking at the postmark, I realized that this piece of mail had taken only seven days to arrive, instead of the ten it normally took to get to Korea from the United States. The fact that it was placed into my hands on Christmas Day astonished me.

I opened the envelope. Inside was a Christmas card from a young couple who I had known in my previous assignment at Fort Sill, Oklahoma. The husband worked in the personnel office. In the days before I left, they had just found out they were expecting their first child. Yet still they thought to mail a card to me. The forethought they showed while immersed in their own happiness brought tears to my eyes.

I held the card in my hands and read their personal note through my tears. They wrote:

"We pray your ministry in Korea brings you, and all those to whom you minister, joy and peace. Have a blessed Christmas and a wonderful new year!"

God caused a husband and his young, pregnant wife to send me a Christmas greeting that fulfilled the purest intent of Christmas: love, joy, hope and peace. It was a parallel to the Christmas story that I just couldn't ignore.

Just as Jesus was Emmanuel—"God with us"—I took this card as a sign of reassurance from God that, although I was unaccompanied by my family on this tour, I was accompanied by God himself. God had neither forsaken me nor forgotten me. He knew exactly where I was, even a world away from my family and my home at Christmas.

A sense of spiritual strength and encouragement came over me that day. I now felt certain that I could endure the hardship of separation over the coming year. After receiving this gift, I was able to offer comfort to many others suffering the same pangs of loneliness. For that, I am eternally grateful, both to this couple and to God himself for his tender mercy and lovingkindness.

Chaplain Michael White began his military career as a chaplain's assistant and spent three years on active duty before he returned to Alabama to pastor churches and serve in the Alabama Army National Guard. He later returned to active duty for almost ten years, after which he returned to pastor in Alabama once again. He and his wife, Ellen, have two children and two grandchildren.

6

A Visit from Lieutenant Dan

CHAPLAIN STEVEN SATTERFIELD

CAPTAIN, COLORADO ARMY NATIONAL GUARD

One of the most rewarding parts of my job here in Afghanistan is to gather and provide supplies for schools and school children. We get boxes of supplies from generous Americans, and from churches, schools and charities. The children are thrilled to get literally anything, from rulers to winter coats. It's a special privilege to help girls in their schooling, because until now women haven't been allowed an education.

One day, we gave out supplies to a local school near our Forward Operating Base (FOB) Finley-Shields in Afghanistan. Later, Officers' Christian Fellowship printed a picture of me handing out the supplies. A retired Army colonel saw the photo and put me in touch with an organization called Operation International Children (OIC).

The thing most people would know about OIC is its co-founder: Gary Sinise, the actor. He and Laura Hillenbrand, the author of *Seabiscuit* and *Unbroken,* started the charity after learning of the poverty and squalor of schools in Iraq and Afghanistan.

Well, Gary Sinise's organization said they would send us 30 boxes of supplies!

After getting the news, I contacted Army Corporal William Seo at FOB Garcia. Corporal Seo heads up Project Help Afghanistan, a nonprofit organization that distributes school supplies and runs literacy and vocational skills programs for adults. I figured he could use the supplies.

I'll let Corporal Seo tell you the rest of the story.

Corporal William Seo, Medic, U. S. Army

In September, I got an e-mail from Chaplain Satterfield saying that I would be receiving supplies from Gary Sinise's OIC. Yes, THE Gary Sinise, Lieutenant Dan from *Forrest Gump*, Detective Mac Taylor of *CSI: NY*.

Chaplain Satterfield knew that I help run a charity for the Afghan people. I started it after I was deployed to Afghanistan and saw how poor the people were. One of the first Afghan patients I treated was an old man who walked in bare feet for three days to have a foot ailment treated. He had no shoes to wear. And I had no shoes to give him. That hurt me. I found myself filled with compassion for the Afghan people.

After hearing from Chaplain Satterfield, I found out that Gary Sinise entertained troops overseas with his Lt. Dan Band. On a whim, I e-mailed him to invite him to the base. "I would like to invite you to fly over to our location and help us distribute your donations to two small schools," I e-mailed.

The next morning I received a response from Mr. Sinise. I could not believe it!

"I will be in country (Afghanistan) from November 21-26th playing three concerts for the troops with my band," he wrote. "Getting out to you may be difficult as they have told me they will not let me do any FOB (forward operating base) hops while I am there."

"This was very disappointing to me, but for security reasons they are saying I cannot," he continued. "I would love nothing better than to come to you and deliver our supplies. So, tell me where you are and how big a deal it is to get to you and I will see if I can nudge the powers that be a little."

A few days later, he wrote again. "I am looking into getting out to you."

How amazing is that? My heart started to pump hard. Mr. Sinise couldn't promise anything, but he said he was looking into it. I knew God was working on this one! From then on, deep in my heart I knew it was already a done deal. I never doubted it.

Eventually, I got word from the Pentagon that they were working at getting Mr. Sinise out to us on November 23rd. Mr. Sinise had time to visit just one school, so we chose Daman Elementary School, which was near our base.

To prepare for the visit, two of my colleagues—Dr. Rafi and Assad—worked with me to pack 125 backpacks with OIC's gifts of school supplies, shoes, clothes, hygiene kits and stuffed animals. We also packed gifts for the teachers, the teachers' children and the owner of the school's land. With donations from OIC and the U.S. Army, we also prepared gifts for the school itself: chalk boards, chalk, soccer balls, air pumps and a new tent for the school.

The morning of November 23rd, our troops headed out to the school. Our commander, Captain Kory Kramer, had invited government officials of Goshta Province to be part of the event, and we knew that Major General Curtis Scaparrotti would be joining us. Our little project was becoming quite a big event!

Due to flight delays, Mr. Sinise was about an hour behind schedule. But pretty soon we heard the helicopter fly in, and he landed. Colonel Ed Shock, chief of the Armed Forces Professional Entertainment Division, was with Mr. Sinise. Mr. Sinise and I had interacted by e-mail so many times that I felt like I had known him for a long time. We shook hands and got down to business.

Dr. Rafi and Assad called out the kids' names on the backpacks and, one by one, each student came through the line and received a backpack. The kids took the backpacks back to their tent classrooms and opened them up right away. They started to giggle and laugh with happiness. It just made my day. I am sure Mr. Sinise felt the same way. I knew Dr. Rafi and Asad were happy, too. We took a big photo with the kids, who were all screaming with joy.

The school children weren't the only ones who got gifts that day. A representative from American Airlines presented me with two tickets to fly free anywhere in the U.S., Mexico, Bermuda, the Caribbean or Canada. Something like this only happens on TV! Having Mr. Sinise there was the grand prize itself, but these tickets were a real surprise. I couldn't wait to tell my wife.

After the Daman visit, Mr. Sinise flew in to our base, and I got to fly along with him. At the base, Major General Scaparrotti gave me his Commander's Coin—an award for military personnel—and Mr. Sinise gave me an autographed *CSI: NY* DVD series. Mr. Sinise had a meet-and-greet with our soldiers and a little time to chat with them before it was time for him to go. I was extremely happy to provide this opportunity to the soldiers who I served with in Afghanistan for a year. Thank you for your great service to our country, my fellow combat friends.

What an amazing day it was! Mr. Sinise was such an inspiration to me. A Hollywood celebrity flew all the way out to us to do a small humanitarian aid project together. I didn't know big celebrities could be so down-to-earth. It was just unbelievable. One simple request by e-mail made all of this happen. When God is involved and willing, nothing is impossible. Thank you, Lord, for letting me have a small part in this!

Chaplain Steven Satterfield is a Colorado Army National Guard chaplain ordained by the Association of Vineyard Churches and endorsed by the National Association of Evangelicals. Before his military career, he was a hospital chaplain and a youth director. In his time with the Army National Guard, he has been deployed to Kuwait, Iraq and Afghanistan.

Corporal William Seo is a medic stationed at Fort Sam Hood, Texas. He and his wife, Min Seon, have two children, Ezrima Haeun and Charis Jooeun. His nonprofit charitable organization, Project Help Afghanistan, can be found online.

7

THE WHISPERED SERVICE

CHAPLAIN HENRY LAMAR HUNT

COLONEL, U.S. ARMY, RETIRED

During my time as an Army chaplain, I conducted many a worship service in the jungles of Vietnam. One time, one of our companies had been without religious services for several days, so I wanted to get to them.

The unit—a company of the 1st Battalion, 5th Cavalry Regiment, 1st Cavalry Division—was in sporadic contact with a North Vietnamese unit and had been for quite a while. I remember the date exactly. It was February 21, 1969.

The operations officer at the Tactical Operations Center had some words of warning for me.

"If you visit the company," he said, "you can't be seen or heard or you will draw fire. Do you understand that?"

I said I understood. I caught a ride on a slick—a Huey helicopter—and was dropped off behind a slight hill. I crawled over the hill and into the company area.

The company commander was a friend of mine. He greeted me in a low voice. I told him that I had come to conduct a worship service. He shook his head and pointed off in one direction.

"The enemy soldiers are right over there," he whispered emphatically. "They're just across that stream, no more than 100 meters away. If you conduct a service, you'll draw enemy fire!"

Because of the danger, he said he couldn't allow me to have a service. I wasn't deterred.

"If I can have a service without making a sound or being seen, will you allow it?" I asked.

Reluctantly, he agreed. He whispered into his radio that "19-er"—the chaplain's call sign—would be at a certain spot within the company's perimeter and that those who could get away, and wanted to, should crawl over there.

Once more, he reminded me of the need for silence and of not being seen. I crawled off to my location.

Within minutes, about twelve to fifteen men began crawling toward me. What a sight! Once we were all gathered, we drew our heads into a tight circle and I began the service.

"Hi, fellows," I whispered. "We are going to have a worship service, but we will have to whisper it. Don't forget and speak out. We don't want anyone to get killed because we are worshipping the Lord."

With that, I whispered a call to worship. Then I asked for prayer requests, and the men whispered their requests. I whispered a pastoral prayer, and they whispered the Lord's Prayer in response. I whispered a brief homily, and then the words of the Lord's Supper: *This is my body which is broken for you. This is my blood which is shed for you. This do in remembrance of me.* I passed the communion wafers around the circle. I poured the wine into a C-ration can and passed it around.

But just before closing, I remembered that I carried mimeographed hymns for my worship services. I reached into my rucksack and pulled out the song for that week and passed the pages around. We began our whispered hymn:

> Blessed Assurance, Jesus is mine.
> Oh what a foretaste of Glory divine.
> Heir of salvation, purchase of God.
> Born of His Spirit, washed in His blood.
> This is my story, this is my song,
> Praising my Savior, all the day long;
> This is my story, this is my song,
> Praising my Savior, all the day long.

Can you imagine? There we were, surrounded by the enemy, in danger of drawing fire, and we whispered, "Blessed Assurance!" It was just the assurance these men needed. I whispered a benediction and we parted. "So long, fellows," I said. "God bless you." I crawled back over the hill to the chopper and the soldiers crawled back to their positions at war.

Since that day, I have preached to dozens and I've preached to thousands. I've preached in a beautiful cathedral and in grand churches. But for me, that whispered service in a Vietnam jungle remains in my memory the most powerful worship experience I have ever had.

Chaplain Henry Lamar Hunt retired from the U.S. Army after 30 years of service. He was a civilian pastor in Florida and South Carolina for ten years before his military career. As a chaplain, he was ordained and endorsed by the Assemblies of God church and later by the United Methodist Church. Among his assignments, he has served in Panama, Korea, Vietnam and Germany. Since 1995, he has pastored a small church near Ocala, Florida. Chaplain Hunt has written two books, Hello God! A Daily Call to Faith and Worship (HLH Ministries, 2001) and Touching the Hand of Jesus (HLH Ministries, 2002), which contain stories of his combat service, including an account of this story. He and his wife, Shirley, have released a CD of their sacred music, Lamar and Shirley Sing. The couple have three children and five grandchildren.

The hymn "Blessed Assurance" was written in 1873 by Fanny Crosby.

8

THE LOSS OF SO MANY

CHAPLAIN GEORGE PUCCIARELLI
CAPTAIN, U. S. NAVY, RETIRED

CHAPLAIN ARNOLD RESNICOFF
CAPTAIN, U.S. NAVY, RETIRED

CHAPLAIN DANNY WHEELER
COMMANDER, U.S. NAVY RESERVE, RETIRED

Early on the morning of October 23, 1983, a suicide bomber drove a delivery truck carrying a payload of powerful explosives down the airport road in Beirut, Lebanon, and plowed into a Marine barracks, killing 241 American Marines, sailors and soldiers. Chaplains George Pucciarelli, Arnold Resnicoff and Danny Wheeler were there.

Chaplain Pucciarelli: It was 6:20 Sunday morning, stand down time. Everybody was just getting up. Rabbi Resnicoff was already awake and brushing his teeth. We heard the explosion and then, even though our building was about 100 yards away, we felt an earthquake strong enough to knock people out of their bunks. A piece of ceiling above me came down, just missing me. The mosquito netting around my bed kept a chunk of it from hitting me in the head.

Chaplain Resnicoff: Most of the Marines ran toward the foxholes and bunkers, thinking the explosion was maybe a single rocket or shell. But Father Pucciarelli and I ran in the direction of the explosion, just in case someone had been wounded. So Pooch and I were among the first to reach the building after the blast.

We faced a scene almost too terrible to describe. The massive four-story building was reduced to a pile of rubble. Clouds of dust, mixed with smoke and fire, obscured our view. Bodies and pieces of bodies were everywhere. We began to hear the screams of the wounded and cries for help from those trapped. The magnitude of the tragedy quickly became apparent, and Marines came running from all directions to help.

Chaplain Pucciarelli: When we got there, at first all you could see was dust, dust all over the ground. But then we saw motion, things moving in the dust. We realized then that we had survivors to get out.

A battalion aid station was set up and we began working our way through the rubble. We found people slumped over, contorted, crying out, people who were deafened from the explosion, guys still in their sleeping bags, either already dead or dying. Marines dug with their hands until they were bloody, trying to free their trapped buddies.

Chaplain Resnicoff: We tore our undershirts to use as bandages and to wipe blood from wounds. We tried to comfort the wounded, but sometimes all we could do was just let them know help was on the way. If it seemed safe to move the wounded, we tried to pull them out and carry them to safety, because they were in danger from the fire and the smothering smoke.

Chaplain Pucciarelli: As we moved among the wounded and the grieving, we were constantly stooping down and picking up things we saw on the ground—letters, wallets, photos—and we took them to a secure spot.

Chaplain Resnicoff: Certain images will stay with me always. I remember a Marine who found a wad of money amidst the rubble. He held it at arm's length as if it were dirty and cried out for a match or a lighter, so that he could burn it. No one wanted to profit from the suffering of the catastrophe. Along with the rest of the men, I was hypnotized and watched as he burned the money.

Throughout this terrible day, the words of the prophet Malachi kept recurring to me, words he spoke some 2,500 years ago as he looked around him and saw fighting and cruelty and pain: *Have we not all one Father? Has not one God created us all?* It was tragically obvious that our world still could not answer that question with a yes.

Still, perhaps some of us could keep the question alive. Father Pucciarelli and I worked that day as brothers. At some point in the day, I realized my kippa, my skullcap, was gone. The last I remember, I had used it to mop someone's brow. Pooch cut a circle out of his cloth camouflage cap for me to use as a head covering. Somehow, we both wanted our Marines to know that we were not just chaplains, but that we were a Christian chaplain and a Jewish chaplain working together side by side.

Chaplain Pucciarelli: Both of us knew that our fellow chaplain, Protestant Chaplain Danny Wheeler, had spent the night in the bombed building. We were afraid that he was dead.

Chaplain Resnicoff: Pooch and I were so sure Danny was dead that we vowed that when the day came to return to the States, we would visit his wife together.

Chaplain Wheeler: I was asleep in my room on the fourth floor when the explosion tore through the building. We had been on high alert and the Marines in my building had been ordered to the basement as a precaution. But the basement was hot and stuffy, and when the order was lifted, many of us returned to our bunks for the night. I had a corner room, and my bunk was beside an inside wall. My chaplain assistant, Corporal John Olson, slept in his bunk next to the window.

I may have been knocked out, I don't know. I came to not knowing what had happened. It was dark, and columns of dust were rising all around me. I had been hit hard in the head, and I was pinned down in a crouched position. I couldn't move my legs. My eardrum had been broken and blood was draining from my ear. I remember being terribly thirsty.

In the darkness, I could see only one tiny pinpoint of light. Slowly, I began to realize what had happened—I had been buried alive!

I tried to lift the concrete off of me, but it came crashing back down. I screamed out loud, trying to get someone's attention, but no one heard me. I was terrified. I didn't want to die. All around me, I heard cries for help—cries from my Marines. I loved them so, and there was nothing I could do for them. I was filled with regret. As the hours went by, I talked to God a lot, but I was angry, even at God. I thought about my family, and about never seeing them again.

Chaplain Pucciarelli: We were walking among the debris, searching for survivors, and a Marine beside me spotted a purple cloth. I knew immediately what it was. It was Danny's Advent stole, one that he wore on Sundays and for special services. His wife had made it for him. I picked it up and hollered down, "Is anybody down there?"

Chaplain Wheeler: I called up, "Yes, I'm here!" It was almost a whisper. I was losing my voice. Somebody said, "We're coming for you!" I could hear them digging. They told me to keep making noise so they could find me. They kept digging and digging. Finally, I felt someone take my hand. I'll never forget that touch.

At one point, the debris shifted and some concrete came crashing down, pushing my head into a cement block and pressing down on my body. I kept praying and saying, "God help me!" I could barely breathe. I felt like I was suffocating.

I prayed, "God, kill me now or let me live." I didn't want to die slowly. After that, I was at peace. I felt God's presence. I knew he would take care of me. I was ready to give up everything. I wasn't afraid.

Chaplain Resnicoff: The digging went on for four hours until they dragged Danny out alive. He later told me that I treated him like a newborn baby when they got him out, counting his fingers and toes, trying to see if he was whole. I didn't realize that I was being so obvious, but the truth was that we could not believe that he was in one piece.

Chaplain Wheeler: I later learned that the wall beside my bed had collapsed in a sort of A-frame over me, which kept me from being crushed. It was a special wall. All the chaplains who had lived there before me had written blessings on that wall and signed their names. We called it the "Blessings Wall." It saved my life.

Chaplain Resnicoff: As they brought over a stretcher for Danny, I hugged him. I can still hear his first words. Racked with pain, still unsure of his own condition, he asked about his assistant. Like so many of the men we saved that day, he asked about others first.

Chaplain Wheeler: After they got me out, I stood up. I didn't have any broken bones, just bruises and a cut on my head. I wanted to search for my assistant, but I collapsed and they got me to a gurney. Pooch folded up my Advent stole and laid it under my head for a pillow as they carried me away. I was glad to be alive. But I was forever changed.

Chaplain Resnicoff: I had arrived in Beirut just two days before the bombing. I was at sea and had been called in to lead a memorial service for a Jewish Marine who had been killed by sniper fire. I stayed for four days afterward. It was a terrible time, the Marines working tirelessly to identify their fallen comrades and prepare them for burial. We comforted them as they grieved. Something as simple as a scrap of paper, a birthday card or a photo of someone's children could set off an avalanche of emotions. Finding a friend's body was almost indescribably heartbreaking.

In Jewish tradition, when we visit the home of a mourner during *shiva*, the week following a loved one's death, we follow a simple rule: If a mourner initiates a conversation, we respond. Otherwise, we sit in silence, communicating concern through our presence, without words. Somehow, I applied the rules of *shiva* during those terrible days of digging. If a Marine or a sailor said something, I responded; otherwise I simply stood by.

Chaplain Pucciarelli: It took five days to extract all the bodies from the building. Marines and sailors endured sniper fire while they worked without regard for their own safety to save as many of their comrades as possible. I wore my stole and anointed the dead with Last Rites for those five days. Most often, there was no way of knowing who the person was or whether they were Catholic or Protestant or Jewish.

Chaplain Wheeler: I was flown to the naval hospital in Naples, Italy, for recovery. While I was there, I asked to see a list of casualties. As I read down through the list, every name on that list hurt me, every name cut me deeply. My assistant, John Olson, was on that list. He was just 21 years old. My physical pain was nothing compared to the psychic emptiness I felt. I loved my battalion. I grieved the loss of so many lives, so many friends, the loss of all those relationships, all those futures.

For many years, I was in a state of shock. I felt like a failure, like I had let my battalion down. I knew I needed help, but I didn't ask for it. Finally, after 15 years of struggling, I was diagnosed with post-traumatic stress syndrome and I got help from two chaplains in Veterans Affairs. I know God called me to go to Beirut, and because of my experience I am good at helping people through times of grief, but to this day I wish it had never happened. I look forward to meeting my friends again someday. I know that I will.

Chaplain Pucciarelli: Over the years, I have repeatedly been asked about this day. Of course, I talked about it at the memorial services I conducted after the bombing. I have revisited it for several anniversary memorial services. Talking about it has been therapeutic. This was the most challenging time of my life, but at the same time, it also proved to me that everything good that represents America is in that uniform we wear.

Chaplain Resnicoff: That October day in Beirut, men reached heroic heights not only of physical endurance and courage, but of sacrifice, compassion, kindness and simple human decency. The Bible tells us that we are created in the image of God. As God's creatures, we have within us the power to reflect the highest values of our Creator. Because of the actions I witnessed during the hell of that time in Beirut, I glimpsed at least a fleeting image of heaven. I saw God's hand in the hearts and hands of men who chose to act as brothers.

Chaplain George Pucciarelli is an ordained Catholic priest from the Diocese of Boston, who served as a U. S. Navy chaplain for the Archdiocese for the Military Services for 30 years. Father Pucciarelli became a Reservist in the Navy Chaplain Corps in 1972 and entered active duty in 1980. He became Chaplain of the U.S. Marine Corps in 1995 and later served as Chaplain for the Naval Security Group. He retired in 2002 and today is parish priest for St. Bernadette's Catholic Church in Hedgesville, West Virginia, where his brother, sister and mother live.

Chaplain Arnold Resnicoff is a retired Navy chaplain and a consultant on interfaith values and interreligious affairs. Rabbi Resnicoff helped create the Vietnam Veterans Memorial, and delivered the closing prayer at its 1982 dedication. After the bombing of the Marine barracks in Beirut, the White House asked him to write about the tragedy. President Ronald Reagan read his report as his keynote address for the Rev. Jerry Falwell's 1984 Baptist Fundamentalism convention in Washington, D.C. He also has served as a special assistant for values and vision for the Secretary and the Chief of Staff of the U.S. Air Force. Rabbi Resnicoff has one daughter, Malka.

Chaplain Danny Wheeler retired in 2008 as a Navy Reserve chaplain endorsed by the Evangelical Lutheran Church in America after 26 years of service. He was a pastor in Wisconsin for five years before his military career. He served many times with the Marines in Okinawa, Japan, as well as with the Marine Corps Reserve Center at the Minneapolis–St. Paul Air Reserve Station. Today, he is pastor of Milltown Lutheran Church in Milltown, Wisconsin. He and his wife, Brenda, have three sons, Andy, Johnny and Ben, and six grandsons, one of whom is with the Lord.

9

SURROUNDED BY SHARKS

CHAPLAIN WALTER BEAN

LIEUTENANT COLONEL, U.S. AIR FORCE

We hold these truths to be self-evident, that all men
are created equal, that they are endowed by their
Creator with certain unalienable Rights, that among
these are Life, Liberty and the pursuit of Happiness.

THE UNITED STATES

DECLARATION OF INDEPENDENCE

Before I went on active duty sixteen years ago, I led a pretty sheltered life. I was the pastor of a small church in northwest Missouri. I had never traveled—I had never even been out of the country.

In 1995, I was deployed to Cuba. I was there to support the migrant camps of so-called "boat people" who had fled Cuba for the United States. If they were intercepted at sea by the Coast Guard, they were sent to the U.S. Naval Station at Guantanamo Bay. The military was there to guard the camps and see that people were being adequately cared for while they were being processed.

When I was there, 80,000 people lived in the camps. Conditions were terrible. People were doing the best they could, but what I saw was horrible. The camps were crowded and dirty. Entire families were crammed into small canvas tents and their only furniture was made from cardboard. Port-a-potties served as toilets and people bathed at a spigot. It was 110 degrees every day I was there.

Each day, I went into the camps and talked to people, just trying to lift their spirits. People told me incredible stories of their desperate attempts to make it to the United States.

One day, I sat down at a picnic table next to a woman with a young boy. She told me this story.

Wanting to escape poverty and political oppression, this woman had arranged and paid dearly for passage for herself and her son. Of course, the group had to travel in darkness, and these boats are not what you'd call yachts. They're small and unstable and crammed with as many people as they can hold. They have no facilities for cooking or toileting. Inevitably, sharks become attracted to the fluids and waste that surround these boats.

During this woman's harrowing journey, sharks began to circle the boat. The seas were heavy and the waves high and the boat was in danger of capsizing. In rising fear, everyone in the boat huddled together and prayed for survival while the dawn approached.

By chance, the Coast Guard spotted the boat and sent out a cutter. But by the time it pulled up, the boat had sunk. Everyone was in the water and people were clinging to debris. This woman was holding tightly onto her son, lifting him up out of the water so that he could breathe. Every time she held him up, she would sink below the waves herself.

Suddenly, she felt a searing pain in her side. *"It's a shark! I've been attacked!"* she thought, gasping from the pain.

Certain that her own death was imminent, she was determined that her son would live. As the Coast Guard began to pluck people out of the water, she kept holding her son high over her head, even though it pushed her below the surface of the water. Waves of searing pain racked her body.

Finally, she couldn't hold her breath any longer. Under the waves, she began to slip into blackness. In a moment, she would lose her grip on her child and both would drown. Just then, a Coast Guardsman snatched her son out of her hands and lifted both mother and child into the boat.

After her rescue, the woman found she hadn't been attacked by a shark, but had been bashed repeatedly by heavy debris flung at her in the waves. She had become tangled in a net and would never have been able to free herself. Without the arrival of her rescuers, death would have been certain.

As I listened to this young mother's story, I realized just what great lengths people will go to in order to escape tyranny and oppression. They will risk their very lives for the smallest chance at freedom.

After telling me her harrowing story, this young woman was eager to talk about life in America. She had so many questions.

"Will the government let me have three gallons of milk instead of two? Will they let me have two pairs of shoes for my son?" she asked me. "Will they throw me in jail if I sell a pair to my neighbor?"

She didn't have the first idea of what it meant to live in a country where she could make her own decisions and enjoy the fruits of her own labor. And yet she had risked everything she had, even her life, to find out.

We are so blessed to live in this country. People are desperate to get here, even if they don't fully understand the freedom and the liberty that we enjoy. It was a great privilege for me to pray with this young mother who dreamed about a new life that she could not even imagine. It has made me appreciate my country in a way that I never did before.

Chaplain Walter Bean is an Air Force chaplain endorsed by the Church of the Nazarene. Prior to his military service, he was a pastor of a church in Missouri. In addition to his service in Cuba, he has been deployed overseas to Turkey, Italy, Japan, South Korea, Pakistan and Iraq. He and his wife, Donna, have three daughters, Caitlin, Allison and Emily.

10

JESUS LOVES YOU!

CHAPLAIN GREGG HAZLETT

LIEUTENANT, U. S. NAVY

About six months ago, while in homeport in Gulfport, Mississippi, I was counseling a Seabee who was suffering major emotional traumas. His marriage was foundering and he and his wife were separated. He had been on several desert deployments to Iraq and Kuwait and hadn't seen his kids in a long time. He was severely depressed and exhibiting a classic borderline personality. He was one troubled young man.

He came into my office one day to talk things out. I had some concerns that he might be suicidal. He seemed to be checking out, so to speak. From his body language, I could see that he wasn't registering anything I said. I tried to elicit a confirmation of any suicidal tendencies, as a chaplain is trained to do, but he wouldn't admit to it.

"Are you going to hurt yourself?" I asked him straight out.

"No, Chaplain, I'm not," he answered.

I wasn't convinced of the truth of his answer. Anyone in the military knows that if you admit to troubles like this, you get scooped up and whisked away to a mental health facility. It can damage your military career forever.

Despite his reluctance to admit his despair, the Seabee made a suicide pact with me. He agreed to stay with a battle buddy that night and to contact me if he felt he was going to do something impulsive. He agreed to come back the next day to talk with me again, and we set up a time and place.

Before he left the office, I prayed for the Seabee. I had never prayed with him before. He didn't come from a religious family, and for him to even come to me to talk was a huge step. I kept my prayer short—I simply asked God to reveal himself to this young man in a powerful and obvious way.

That night, the Seabee skipped out on his battle buddy. He went to the store and bought a bottle of sleeping pills with the intent of ending his life. It was late in the evening, and already dark. He got into his car and began the drive home. Along the way, he stopped at a red light. While waiting, he heard the blare of an insistent car horn. Startled, he looked around.

In the next lane over, a driver was urgently honking his horn. Confused, the Seabee rolled down his window. The other driver rolled down his.

"I know you are hurting, but Jesus loves you!" the other driver hollered over.

The light turned green and the driver took off.

The Seabee was so shocked he couldn't carry out his plan. The driver wasn't anyone he knew or recognized. He came to my office the next day and checked himself into a treatment center. He is still alive today. All I can say is, Praise God!

Chaplain Gregg Hazlett is endorsed by the National Association of Evangelicals and has served with a Naval Mobile Construction Battalion deployed to Afghanistan. He was a youth pastor for ten years, specializing in outdoor education ministries, and he was a policeman for five years prior to entering the military. He and his wife, Joanna, have an infant son, Ethan.

11

TRACKED DOWN

CHAPLAIN CHRISTOPHER REEDER

CAPTAIN, U.S. AIR FORCE

How many people can say they met their wife in Afghanistan? I know, usually when you deploy to Afghanistan, you bring back a rug.

In 2006, I was set to be loaned out to the Army for five months and deploy to Afghanistan. One day in May, my parents attended a National Day of Prayer service at their church, Germantown Baptist Church near Memphis, Tennessee. Before the service began, my mom and dad went up to the pastor to ask a favor.

"Our son Chris is a chaplain in the Air Force, and he's about to deploy to Afghanistan. Would you pray for him?" they asked.

Of course, my parents suspected that the pastor might do what most people do, and say, "Sure, fine, no problem" and then just forget about it. Well, he didn't forget about it. During the service, he brought them up on the podium and introduced them.

"This is Penny and Kerry Reeder," he said. "Their son Chris is a chaplain in the Air Force and he's about to deploy to Afghanistan. Let's pray for him."

After the service ended, a young woman who worked at the church greeted them. She asked a sly question.

"Is your son's family deploying with him?" she asked my parents.

Well, of course my parents answered that I wasn't married and didn't have a family. That was just the information she was after.

This young woman—her name was Jen—wasn't put off by the idea of the chaplain son being deployed to Afghanistan. She had grown up overseas in a missionary family and had lived in India and Thailand. She had been to Afghanistan a few times. And, she had in fact just accepted a job teaching at the International School of Kabul.

Jen decided to see if could manage to run into Chaplain Reeder sometime. So, after she arrived in Afghanistan, she kept her ears open.

One day, the director from her school met two agents from OSI and NCIS. You may be familiar with NCIS from the television show. Every service has the equivalent of an FBI-type of force tasked with investigating felony crimes. In the Army they're called the Criminal Investigation Division (CID); in the Navy they're called NCIS (Naval Criminal Investigation Service); and in the Air Force they're the Office of Special Investigations (OSI). The director of the school invited the agents to go hiking with them, and they set a date.

The day for the hiking trip arrived, and guess who came along? Jen ended up in the same truck with the OSI and NCIS agents. When she discovered their military affiliation, she asked her second strategic question.

"Do you know a chaplain named Chris Reeder?" she asked.

"No," they said. "But we can find him for you."

That afternoon, the two agents walked into the chapel at Camp Phoenix in Kabul. I was in the back office at the time, working with our other chaplains.

One thing you need to know about OSI and NCIS is that if they come looking for you, it's not a good day. And so here these two guys walk in and they say, "We're from OSI and NCIS, and we're looking for Chris Reeder!"

Well, of course, every head in that room popped up and looked straight at me, which completely denied me the opportunity to say, "Umm . . . well . . . sorry. He just left."

"Fellas, can we go outside and talk?" I asked them.

We went outside and they started in.

"Do you know a girl named Jennifer Ollis?" one of them asked.

"No, sir, I've never laid eyes—or hands, or anything else—on anyone named Jennifer Ollis," I said emphatically. "I don't know what you're talking about."

"Relax, Chaplain," he said. "It's nothing like that."

They brought me up to speed on the girl who wanted to meet me. I met them halfway. I gave them my e-mail address and said they could pass it on if they liked. I just figured they would never see this girl—whoever she was!—again.

I was in no hurry to meet anyone. For years, I had a mental list in my head of what I was looking for in a wife. I made a list because I had the worst radar for women in the world. If there was a messed-up girl within a fifty-mile radius, I would seek her out like a missile! I had even quit dating for about the previous five years.

I could have been single for the rest of my life and been just fine, but I just didn't feel like God was calling me to life as a single. In my prayers, I said to him, *"God, if you have somebody out there for me, you're going to have to introduce her to me. And you're going to have to do it in a*

way that's perfectly obvious that it's from Your hand. You're going to have
to hit me over the head with a ton of bricks."

After I had arrived at the base in Afghanistan, another chaplain there asked me to write down my "wife wish list" and said he would pray through that list with me. My list had 28 items, everything from "born-again, conservative Christian" to "if she has a dog, she'll keep it outside."

Well, about two or three weeks after we started praying through my list, I got my first e-mail from Jen.

The very same day the agents came to see me at the chapel, they ran into Jen that night at a coffeehouse in Kabul and gave her my information. So, within about 12 hours, this girl I didn't know had sicced the OSI and NCIS on me, they'd tracked me down, *and* they'd reported back to her!

Jen and I started trading emails. One of the things that really impressed me was the way she talked about God. She always said "Father." Not "Father God" or "God our Father." It was always just "Father." There was something really intimate about the way she talked about God, and I could tell by the way it was written that she felt like God was really a Father to her.

"I want to get to know this girl's faith," I said to myself. I invited her to come to our chapel services on the base.

It is true that this girl's faith was what first attracted me to her. I had no idea what Jen looked like. I had never seen a picture of her. I had in mind a thin brunette for my wife, but I hadn't asked those kinds of questions in my e-mails.

The first day Jen came for a chapel service, she arrived with a girlfriend. I went out to the gate to meet them.

At the gate, the two girls walked in side-by-side. They were all wrapped up in coats and their heads were covered, and I didn't know which one was which. One of the girls was blonde and the other was a starving-artist-looking brunette—the kind I'd always gone for. I looked at her and then I looked back at the blonde girl, and I said to myself: *"That's her. That's Jen."* And I knew. I knew she would change my life. God had hit me with that ton of bricks.

Jen and I saw each other about a half dozen times before my deployment ended. On July 5, 2008, after an 18-month long-distance romance, Jen and I were married at a chapel on Eglin Air Force Base in Florida. We kissed for the first time when the pastor said, *"You may now kiss the bride."* Now I'm preparing for my second deployment. I should be gone for about four months, and then I get to come home to my bride—back home to the girl who had criminal investigators track me down! Back home to the girl with the incredible faith.

Chaplain Christopher Reeder is ordained and endorsed by the Associate Reformed Presbyterian Church. He has been a chaplain since 2004 and has served at Eglin Air Force Base in Florida and Andrews Air Force Base in Maryland. He and Jennifer have been married for two years.

12

GIVE ME JESUS

CHAPLAIN STEVEN SCHAICK

COLONEL, U.S. AIR FORCE

Everyone who calls on the name of the Lord will be saved.

JOEL 2:32

One of the great privileges of being a chaplain is to enter into the very personal and sacred parts of the lives of others. When warriors come to me with their hurt and their pain, the heart's cry I hear most often is not, "Fix my life," "Get me out of here," or "I hate it here!" but simply, "Give me Jesus."

The day I left for Afghanistan on my latest deployment, my wife and I were enjoying a few last-minute hugs at the airport. Near us, we noticed another family clearly bidding farewell to their husband and father. The soldier's wife, fighting back tears, was snapping as many pictures as she could of daddy with his little girls—one of whom was in a wheelchair. Her photos would be loving reminders of this family's hero when he was so very far from home.

With one final hug, we both let go of our families at the same time and headed for the gate. The two of us, complete strangers only moments ago, already shared a powerful bond. As we were walking to the aircraft I said to him, "You have a beautiful family."

"It just never seems to get any easier," he said. He looked at me with tears forming and simply shook his head. Had he tried to continue speaking, nothing but sobs would have come out. He and I became good friends as we made our long journey together. In our conversation, in our sharing of family stories, in our lamenting of the long deployment ahead, we could not avoid talking about faith, and in talking about faith, we could not avoid Jesus.

This heartbroken warrior told me, in his own way, that there was only one way he would ever be able to focus on the task at hand and know for certain that his wife would find the strength and courage to single-parent her way through the next four months. His cry was not for a change in circumstances. His cry was for Jesus. Give me Jesus. Give my wife and three children Jesus.

On the flight from Frankfurt, Germany, to Incirlik, Turkey, I began talking with a six-foot three-inch Army Sergeant First Class who crammed himself into the tiny seat to my left. He and I shared small talk until he figured out that I was a chaplain. That's when our small talk turned to heart talk.

His was not the three-month deployment I was dreading, but an 18-month tour of duty. As if that were not enough, this grieving sergeant told me of his pregnant daughter who was living with a guy twice her age and of his high school-aged son who was struggling with overwhelming anger. And, to top it off, his wife of twenty years told him—as he was leaving—that she would probably not be there when he returned. She just couldn't take it anymore.

As this bright and articulate non-commissioned officer told me his story, through his pain and regret I heard loud and clear his cry for a miracle. I heard his longing for someone to tell him that everything was going to be okay. I heard him ask for all the things that only a Savior can give. I heard him say, Give me Jesus.

During my deployment, a soldier named Jake and I hit it off after he began coming regularly into the chapel tent for coffee and snacks. This good-looking young man and I shared an instant bond—we were both Cheeseheads from Wisconsin! Jake was somewhat timid when he first began to come by the chapel. He'd grab his coffee and a cookie or two and then leave.

One day, though, he stayed awhile and poured his heart out to me. He told me of his life back home, how he and his young bride cared for a reclusive neighbor who seemed to carry with him more anger than he could deal with. He told me of his exemplary leadership skills and how he'd been so very successful in the military. But then Jake told me the real reason he was talking with me.

Recently, Jake said, he had left his weapon in the DFAC (dining facility). This may not sound like a big deal, but what he did is one of the biggest infractions of the U.S. military. A soldier and his weapon are joined at the hip and never to be parted. He told me how ashamed he was. He cried and lamented his error. He begged for forgiveness. He pleaded for mercy. He desperately wanted one more chance to prove himself a faithful soldier.

As Jake's tearful cries died away, the chapel became silent. In the silence, I prayed for this young soldier. I prayed that Jesus would show himself as Divine Agent and that this situation would one day be an impetus for Jake's thanks and praise. For my friend who was too broken to pray for himself, I prayed, Give him Jesus.

Several months later, I got an e-mail from Jake. After his infraction, he said, he was called to his commander's office to be issued a disciplinary Article 15 for leaving his weapon. Standing at attention, sick at heart, he awaited the dreadful judgment. Solemnly, the commander paused, looked Jake squarely in the eyes and said, "Son, I think you've had punishment enough. I'm not going to sign this." He tore up the Article 15 and sent my friend on his way.

Jake and I had prayed, Give me Jesus.

A prayer for mercy will always be answered. Not one of us has a problem, a concern, a regret, a pain, an illness, a trouble, a burden, a difficulty, a dilemma, a quandary, a crisis, a predicament, an emergency, a disaster, a calamity, or a catastrophe that Jesus cannot handle. You can't "out-need" the loving arms of Jesus. He is waiting to hear that sweet cry of a broken heart—Give me Jesus!

Chaplain Steven Schaick is an Air Force chaplain endorsed by the Presbyterian Church (USA). Prior to the chaplaincy, he was associate pastor of Mt. Zion Church in Beavercreek, Ohio. Before that, he served as an F-15 Integrated Avionics Specialist for the Air Force. He and his wife, Denise, have two children, Elizabeth and Nathan.

13

THE HAND OF GOD

CHAPLAIN TIMOTHY BOHR

MAJOR, U.S. ARMY RESERVE

The first warning that our camp was under attack came when we heard the explosion of a mortar shell. It was the middle of the night and we were all sound asleep. It might be more accurate to say we dreamed the explosion.

A second explosion sounded, this one closer. Then, a third one, closer still. We scrambled in the darkness for our boots, helmets and body armor. As we ran from the barracks to our rally point, we could see a blaze about a half mile away. Several barracks tents were on fire. Others were riddled with shrapnel, the fabric shredded like Swiss cheese.

Providentially, the tents were still under construction and no one had moved into them yet. If anyone had been sleeping there that night, some would surely have gone home in body bags.

That mortar and rocket attack confirmed to us that this region of Iraq, ten miles from Fallujah, was an active war zone in 2003. I was assigned to the Blackhawk helicopter battalion of the 82nd Airborne

Division, which was conducting security and stabilization operations until the Marines could arrive and take over.

It is hard to capture in words what it is like to live in a war zone. Pictures on TV provide some idea, but the remote control prevents any real empathy. You have to be there to really understand it.

After an attack like this one, I made it a habit to visit tents after the smoke had cleared. Soldiers often expressed amazement that I, as a chaplain, didn't carry a weapon. They couldn't conceive of being unarmed in a combat zone.

"Aren't you afraid?" they would ask.

"No, I'm not," I would say. "Can I tell you why?"

One time a soldier wanted to hear the answer, and I pulled a small New Testament out of my side leg pocket—a pocket usually used for ammo. It was as if I had pulled out a live grenade.

"He's got a Bible!" came the cry from his buddies as they scattered. They wanted God on their side, but not too close.

I can honestly say I had no fear. My life was in God's hands. It was not the enemy who would choose the time of my death. That question was in the hands of my Heavenly Father.

That doesn't mean that I did not suffer or grieve with my fellow soldiers. With every day, the mounting casualties of the battalions and units around us tested our resolve. Many began to face their own mortality and search the condition of their souls.

One day we got a call that a Chinook helicopter had been shot down. My battalion sent out a first response team to secure the crash site and provide medical aid.

All we could do at camp was wait for the team to return. Even more than the mortar attacks, this downing of a helicopter hit home the hardest for my pilots and crew chiefs. They flew daily missions—it could easily have been any one of them.

We expected that we would receive and treat the survivors of the crash. But they were so badly injured that they were all flown directly to the main hospital in Baghdad.

Instead, soldiers from a second Chinook that had been flying tandem with the one shot down were flown to our camp. When they arrived, their uniforms were stained with dirt and blood from the bodies of their fellow soldiers, which they had helped pull from the burning wreckage.

We chaplains went from bed to bed, offering what comfort we could. A prayer, an encouraging word, a listening ear. That's what we could offer, while our staff provided hot showers, clean clothes, hot meals, and a place to sleep.

The medical staff asked me to sit with a soldier they feared was a suicide risk. One of his buddies had been on the downed Chinook—we later found out his friend had died. Earlier, he had lost another friend and had been wounded himself in an attack while out on patrol.

For over an hour I sat with this soldier on a cot in a back room, my arm around his shoulder. He was in shock, severely traumatized. We didn't say much, mostly just stared at the wall. He didn't cry, but I cried inwardly for him. Finally, I prayed with him and turned him over to the doctors' care.

It was almost dark when I made my way back to my quarters. Along the way, I stopped in to visit our medics who had been on the first response team. Although this was their job, what they were trained to do, they were shaken.

One of the medics in particular sought me out. In all likelihood, he had saved the lives of a dozen soldiers who would have died without his care. He wanted to talk with me privately. We went outside, into the cool, dark desert air, and leaned against a Humvee ambulance.

"Chaplain," he began, "I saw some things today that I haven't told anyone about. But I need to talk with someone. Would you be willing to listen?"

With that, he began to describe to me, in graphic detail, what he had seen that day. He described the condition of the bodies he had worked on, the smell of the burning crash site, the horror of the scene.

I wept with the medic at the tragedy of it, our arms around each other in sorrowful embrace. Using the words of the ancient Jewish prayer of blessing, I prayed for God's peace to comfort him.

The Lord bless you and keep you. The Lord make His face shine upon you, and be gracious unto you. The Lord lift up His countenance upon you, and give you peace.

My heart went out to this soldier, and I loved him. He represented every soldier I had been privileged to touch that day. I loved him for doing his duty under horrific circumstances. I loved him for his humanity and his tears for the fallen. I loved him because he was loved by God.

During those days in the Iraqi desert, the providential hand of God became very real to me. I found the words of the Psalmist to be utterly true.

> *Where can I go from your Spirit?*
> *Where can I flee from your presence?*
> *If I go up to the heavens, you are there;*
> *If I make my bed in the depths, you are there.*
> *If I rise on the wings of the dawn,*
> *If I settle on the far side of the sea,*
> *Even there your hand will guide me,*
> *Your right hand will hold me fast.* (Ps. 139:7–10)

In the midst of an Iraqi desert, I was privileged to be the hand of God on the shoulders of soldiers who desperately needed to know his peace. And through it all I saw his hand of providence guiding me and holding me fast. I am filled with his praise.

Chaplain Timothy Bohr is a U.S. Army Reserve chaplain of dual Canadian and American citizenship ordained by the Evangelical Churches of North America and endorsed by the National Association of Evangelicals. He was mobilized for a year with the 82nd Airborne Division and deployed to Iraq in 2003. He currently provides support programs for at-risk youth and street children as director of youth services for Chilliwack Community Services in Chilliwack, British Columbia. He and his wife, Janice, have two sons, Joshua and Rylan.

14

DID I REALLY CUSS?

CHAPLAIN BILLY BAUGHAM

MAJOR, U.S. ARMY, RETIRED

Oh, break my life if need must be.

No longer mine, I give it Thee.

Oh, break my will; the off'ring take,

For blessing comes when Thou dost break.

ROBERT REYNOLDS JONES, JR., "BROKEN THINGS"

On one overseas assignment, I worked for a commander as his unit chaplain. We had a good relationship, as did my wife with the commander's wife.

This commander was a hard-driven man; he was on the list for promotion to "full-bird" colonel, a rank known by its silver eagle insignia. He was determined to get this promotion—absolutely no one was going to stand in his way.

This man truly cared for his soldiers, but he had a big problem: his language. It was rough, to put it mildly. There was not a moment in his conversation that he did not use vulgar language. If you didn't like it, well, he just didn't care.

Our staff consisted of the usual personnel—intelligence officer, physician, chaplain, public relations officer, operations officer, records officer and ordnance commander, among others. Everyone on staff was male, except for one female officer. She was a faithful chapel member, and a strong and dedicated Christian.

Like many others in the service, she tolerated the general profanity you encounter in any military setting. At one meeting, however, her patience gave out. The commander was angry about an event his unit had to attend and he went off.

"I want every [expletive] to be present for this function!" he shouted.

"Sir, with all due respect," the female officer responded, "I don't have the body part you refer to and your comment is offensive to me."

The commander was caught off guard. For a moment, he was speechless, but then he recovered.

"Chaplain," he roared, "I want you in my office after the meeting!"

I was apprehensive, to say the least. When this commander was angry and called officers in, they normally came out with their heads on a platter. But I didn't have a choice. I reported to his office as ordered.

The commander told me he wanted to punish the female officer for her conduct.

"Chaplain," he said, "did you or anyone on the staff put this officer up to her remark?"

"No, sir," I replied. "I believe it was a spontaneous reaction on her part."

"Well, I'm not going to tolerate this [expletive] embarrassment from any staffer of mine!" he roared. "She will be reprimanded."

In the past, I had mentioned the commander's language to him. Regardless of the female officer's presence on staff, even some of the male officers blanched at his language. I decided to hit him with an idea I knew would mean something to him.

"Sir, what you said would be offensive to any female, especially in the company of men. You say these things in her presence repeatedly. When you say such things, the men often snicker and that embarrasses her," I said. "I don't think you purposely intend to do that—it's just your language habit.

"But, sir, you might want to consider that she could bring you up on sexual harassment charges," I continued. "If she reports you, your promotion to colonel would surely be jeopardized. She has no wish to do that, but it is something to consider."

The commander was stunned. He lowered his head into his hands. He was silent for a long time. The silence was deafening—I waited, aware only of some sounds of clanging and banging coming from the nearby Arms Room. I thought for sure that I had gone too far, and that this was it for me. I prepared to take my platter.

Instead, the commander lifted his head and looked up at me.

"Chaplain," he said, quietly, "would you help me stop my [expletive] swearing?"

Boldly, I challenged him.

"For starters, sir," I said, "I recommend that you ask your question again without using an expletive."

Taken by surprise, the commander responded with double the expletives.

I paused and smiled.

"Sir, can you recall specifically what you just said?" I asked him.

He thought for a moment. "Did I really cuss both times?" he asked warily.

I gave the commander some recommendations on how to break his habit of swearing. I invited him to my chapel services and reminded him that the Lord himself befriended Roman commanders. He agreed to come.

The commander was true to his word. He and his wife were there at my very next service. While in our subsequent conversations he seemed open to change, he asked for time to "get religion." Of course, I pointed him to Christ rather than religion.

Over the next few months, I witnessed a new, warm attitude come over the commander. He made joyful noises singing the Sunday morning hymns. We talked from time to time about what Christianity was all about. He was a hardened soldier, but I believe he trusted Christ as his Savior in his own private way.

By the time I left the assignment, the commander's entire demeanor had changed. During those few months, I never once heard him curse again. This pervasive habit was defeated by the power of God working in his heart. In his defeat, the Lord gave him real victory. And, in the end, the commander got his promotion.

Chaplain Billy Baugham retired from active duty as an Army chaplain in 1985. Upon his retirement, Dr. Baugham was elected president of the

Associated Gospel Churches and chairman of its Commission on Chaplains. He also serves as executive director of the International Conference of Evangelical Chaplain Endorsers (ICECE). "Did I Really Cuss?" is excerpted and adapted with permission from the January 2010 issue of the AGC Chaplain Ministry Report newsletter.

15

PING PONG BUDDIES

CHAPLAIN CHAD BELLAMY

CAPTAIN, U.S. AIR FORCE

My first assignment as a military chaplain took me to McGuire Air Force Base in New Jersey. I was so new to the military that I couldn't tell what planes were in the air and what all the rank insignia meant. My highest goal at first was just to make sure I saluted the right people!

So, maybe it was with the eye of the outsider that I came to notice the munitions flight of the maintenance group that I was assigned to. This is the group of people responsible for packing the bullets and preparing the payload. Their job is a thankless one. It's the pilots who get all the glory, while they get left behind on the ground.

Because of the dangerous nature of the work—and the potential for something to go horribly wrong—the munitions flight was isolated from the rest of the Wing. They were tucked away in a secure area, at the end of a road, far away from the day-to-day operations of the base, behind a barrier of trees, dirt walls and a wired gate. To visit, you'd have to approach the security camera at the gate, hit a speaker button and request entrance before they would open the gate for you. It was a little world unto itself, almost a leper colony. If you weren't part of the flight, you never thought about them. In fact, you were thankful not to *be* them.

I went down there one Friday afternoon, just to introduce myself. As they were showing me around, I noticed an unused ping pong table pushed aside in one area. Now, I love sports, rivalry and competition. When I mentioned the table, one of the guys suggested we could play sometime if I wanted to.

"Let's play right now!" I said.

I think my skill level was a little better than they expected from a chaplain. Nobody argued when I said, "Hey, I'll be back next Friday." From then on, whenever I'd approach the gate, I'd hear them shout, "The chaplain's here—get the table out!"

It wasn't long before we had a regular gig going. As the airmen got to know me and trust me, they started coming to me with their concerns. "Hey, you got a minute?" was something I began to hear during my visits.

One senior airman in particular was in the midst of a genuine life crisis, despite her young age. She was barely out of her teens and facing a transition for which she was poorly equipped. She was starting to think that there had to be more to life than partying, but she wasn't sure what. She questioned whether she should be in the military, but didn't know what else there was for her. At one time, she had been guided through life by her faith, but that was a distant memory.

The senior airman was newly married and her husband was also active duty Air Force. Sometimes young servicemen and women marry for the wrong reasons—you're paid more if you're married and you get to move out of the dorms and into married housing in the community. She was struggling to make her marriage work.

Over the next few months, the senior airman visited my office on many occasions. We talked about making choices in life that reap rewards rather than regrets down the road. Many times, my words seemed insufficient for her needs, but I trusted that I was in some small way showing her God at work.

Unexpectedly, in November 2005, my family and I were issued a permanent change of station to Schriever Air Force Base in Colorado. I was sorry to leave my ministry at McGuire, especially my ping pong buddies at the munitions flight.

In Colorado, we settled in and got involved in a local church, quickly becoming part of a small group. Over time, we developed a close friendship with the retired couple who hosted the group at their home and had a real heart for ministering to active duty military personnel.

One day, they mentioned that they were trying to sell a home they owned in the small Pennsylvania town in which they had been raised. The real estate market was tough and the house wasn't selling. Our small group began to pray for them in this situation.

In time, they were pleased to report that they had an offer on the house. The offer came from neighbors they had known for years. The two parties agreed on a purchase price, and the couple flew to Pennsylvania to close the deal. When they returned to Colorado, they told us this story.

The day came for everyone to gather for the closing. The neighbors were there with their daughter, for whom they were buying the house. Our small group leaders had known the daughter as a young child.

Before the closing began, our friends chatted and caught up with their neighbors, and asked the young woman about her life. She told them she was separating from the military and returning to live in her home town. She spoke about her time in the Air Force and, eventually, mentioned that she had worked for a munitions flight at McGuire AFB. She spoke warmly about a chaplain there who had helped her through a difficult period in her life and how devastated she was when he and his family left the base for an assignment at Schriever AFB.

Our friends looked at each other in surprise.

"Could you describe the chaplain to us?" they asked. She was puzzled, but she went on to describe a tall chaplain with red hair, blue eyes and an outgoing personality. She described . . . me!

The "coincidence" discovered, the young woman shared excitedly how our conversations had helped her work through some of life's biggest questions, how my prayers for her had grounded her in faith and driven out her fear. She and her husband were expecting a child, and she felt she was finally on a good path in life.

Amazed, I listened to my friends tell their story. It was so vivid for me that I felt like I was right there with them at the closing, like I was standing in front of this young woman and sharing in her excitement about her new life.

As a chaplain, you rarely get to experience the fruits of your labor. Your job can be as thankless as that of the munitions flight. But God does indeed order our steps. Nothing we do in his name is ever in vain. The world is a small place, and when we sow seeds of God's love into the lives of others, we just never know where the flowers will bloom. Thank you, Lord, for this timely word of encouragement. You know just what we need when we need it.

Chaplain Chad Bellamy was a youth pastor for ten years at churches in Virginia, North Carolina and Georgia before he entered the Air Force in 2002 as a chaplain endorsed by the International Pentecostal Holiness Church. He has served on bases in New Jersey, Colorado, Texas and England. He and his wife, Jeri, have three children.

16

A SORROWFUL SACRIFICE

CHAPLAIN EDDIE BARNETT

LIEUTENANT COLONEL, U.S. ARMY

I walked a mile with Sorrow,

And ne'er a word said she;

But, oh, the things I learned from her

When Sorrow walked with me!

ROBERT BROWNING HAMILTON,

"ALONG THE ROAD"

One day, I talked with a soldier about Abraham and Ishmael. That conversation may have saved my life.

On December 21, 2004, I was getting ready to head to the dining facility for lunch at Forward Operating Base Marez in Mosul, Iraq. I was stopped by a soldier who wanted to talk about Abraham and Ishmael, his son by Sarah's servant Hagar. This biblical story often divides Christians and Muslims. In the Old Testament, God leads Abraham to a remote mountaintop, taking along his beloved son Isaac as the presumed human sacrifice. But in some Islamic traditions, it is not Isaac but Ishmael whom Abraham chooses.

The soldier had squad duties to attend to, so our conversation was brief. But as it turns out, it was just long enough.

After we finished, I headed over to the dining facility. It was a large, sturdy tent that could accommodate hundreds of soldiers. We were in the process of building a concrete mess hall in a more secure area, as FOB Marez had been the target of frequent mortar attacks, and the DFAC was a definite target. We needed to provide more safety for our soldiers. For now, this tent-like structure was all we had.

I got within 15 yards of the tent when a huge explosion ripped through it. I was behind some tall, concrete T-Walls, so I didn't see the explosion so much as hear it. It blew a huge hole in the roof of the tent, and I saw it collapse inward. Then, I heard screams coming from inside the tent, and soldiers began streaming out.

We didn't know what had happened. It could have been a rocket or a mortar attack, as we had been the target of both. There was no way to even know if the attack was over. I had a choice to make—get out of there immediately, or go inside the tent. I walked into the tent.

Inside, it was horrific. Tables and chairs were overturned, food and blood splattered everywhere. Worst of all was the carnage of the dead, the dying and the wounded. Soldiers were thrown to the ground and writhing in pain. I saw one soldier with his face blown off. Bodies lay everywhere.

Then the shock of the explosion hit me, and I froze. In that moment I prayed. "God, give me the strength to do what needs to be done," I asked.

My fellow soldiers had already plunged into their grim tasks. They began helping the wounded out of the tent and over to the nearest hospital, which thankfully was just a few hundred yards away. I joined in, caring for and praying over the wounded. They lined up the bodies of the dead soldiers outside the tent, and I was asked to attend to the dead.

I went down the line of the fallen, soldier after soldier, praying over each one. "Lord God, graciously receive my fellow soldier. Guide him on his life's eternal journey into Your loving arms. In Your grace, please comfort his family," I prayed.

In all, 22 people were killed that day—18 of which were Americans—and more than 60 were wounded. Two soldiers from our battalion died. A Sunni insurgent disguised in an Iraqi military uniform snuck into the mess tent and blew himself up. The explosion ripped around the tent, its deadly shrapnel and searing fireball accomplishing its savage mission.

It is a paradox of war that you experience not only the worst that humanity can be, but the best humanity can be. That day, I saw firsthand the courage and selflessness of the American soldier. Soldier helping soldier, giving and receiving comfort and hope, all pettiness and personal animosities tossed out the window. Amid the horrible suffering of that attack, I saw the spirit of God pervading the darkness.

Chaplain Eddie Barnett was endorsed in 1997 as a United Methodist chaplain and has served in the U.S. Army since then. He has been deployed twice to Iraq, first as battalion chaplain to the Army National Guard's 276th Engineer Battalion and then as brigade chaplain for the 116th Infantry Brigade combat team. Before his military service, he was a credit manager for a division of Goodyear, and he served several pastoral appointments in Virginia. He and his wife, Melinda, have one son, Brian.

17

A Fateful Fireguard

CHAPLAIN JOSEPH LAWHORN
CAPTAIN, U.S. ARMY

CHAPLAIN JOHN ROUTZAHN
LIEUTENANT COLONEL, U.S. ARMY

Greetings Chaplain Routzahn!

I pray this letter finds you well on all accounts. I have thought about you often since our time together in the 1990s at Fort Leonard Wood in Missouri.

I came to basic training a mixed up, wayward soul. My parents divorced when I was young and my mom moved us from Cincinnati to Florida. Although I'd been a good kid, a good student and an athlete, as a teenager I just lost control. Drugs, alcohol, driving under the influence—every dangerous behavior you can think of, I did it. I drifted from job to job—restaurants, construction, carpentry, masonry, bowling alleys, door-to-door sales—whatever I could do just to buy my drugs and alcohol. On my eighteenth birthday, I nearly lost my life in a car wreck.

I had my own apartment on the beach in Florida. I loved that apartment. What I remember most about it is the living room carpet. It was fire-engine red. One day—and I don't remember what happened to bring this on—but one day I remember finally realizing that if I kept on going the way I was, I would end up dead or in jail. I knelt on all fours on the floor, sobbing into that red carpet. "God!" I cried out. "Take over my life. I'm making a mess of it."

Not long after, I came in contact with an Army recruiter and I joined up. Pretty soon I found myself in boot camp at "Fort Lost in the Woods." As you know, in boot camp, you don't have a lot of free time. But it seemed that every time I had a moment to myself, or found myself on guard duty or clean-up detail, there you were. Perhaps you sensed the Holy Spirit's leading in my life and were simply being obedient to God's word. For whatever reason, it seemed you took a special interest in me.

One time, in the middle of the night, I pulled fireguard duty and you came around at two o'clock in the morning and shared the gospel with me. You gave me a little camouflage Bible that night. I still have that Bible to this day.

Over the next two months, our paths just kept crossing. On Sundays, anybody who wanted to worship was given a few hours off. Well, mysteriously, everybody suddenly became very spiritual, because it meant that you could go off to church instead of doing some menial job! My eyes gradually were opened, and you seemed to pounce at each opportunity to spend time with me. After every service, you somehow "needed" a couple of guys to help clean up the chapel and I always stayed. You treated us to snacks and just gave us some down time to shoot the breeze.

Although I had given over my life to Christ there on that red carpet in my apartment, as God worked in my life I wanted to be more formal about my decision. During your Thanksgiving service in 1992, I openly gave my life to Christ and you baptized me in front of the congregation. It's ironic that while basic training is generally a miserable experience, I was on cloud nine! I felt a door was opening for me. I wasn't heading for a dead end any longer. God had a plan for me.

After boot camp ended, I never saw or heard from you again. But you were always on my mind. I have shared with countless people the impact you had on my life. And I've had plenty of opportunity to do so. I have had an incredible Army journey.

During my first enlistment, I applied for and received a "Green to Gold" scholarship, and got to go to college even though I had dropped out of school in the ninth grade. I was commissioned as an infantry officer and got to do it all—Airborne, Ranger, mountaineering, and all the rest. I was the kind of guy trained to jump out of airplanes, kick in the door of an airfield and take out the bad guys. After that, I transferred to the Adjutant General's Corps and got to be a platoon leader and company commander. I even served as an instructor in the AG career course. I have been in lots of leadership positions where I have had the chance to tell my story of salvation.

Eventually, I became even more serious about my walk with Christ and I sensed God calling me into the ministry. In 2006, I resigned my commission and left active duty to attend seminary. In the fall of 2009, I was accepted into the Army Chaplain Corps and I am looking forward to my ministry as a military chaplain.

Throughout my Army career, I have had countless chances to tell soldiers of every rank my story. Whenever I speak of my basic training experience, the name "Chaplain Routzahn" invariably comes up.

I know the impact a chaplain can have on soldiers, because I know firsthand the difference you made in my life. Our time together at Fort Leonard Wood has always held a special place in my heart. God has used my experience with you to help me counsel and minister to many soldiers under my care. It is my dream to someday pull duty with another wayward soul on fireguard, share the Good News of Jesus, and perhaps even give them their first Army camouflage Bible!

Bless you, bless you and bless you, Chaplain Routzahn, for your willingness to make an eternal difference in my life. And, thank you!

Very Respectfully and Sincerely,
CH CPT Joe Lawhorn

Chaplain Joseph Lawhorn served for 11 years on active duty with the U.S. Army and is now an Army chaplain ordained and endorsed by Grace Churches International. He and his wife, Kristen, have four children; Luke, Grace, Ava and Megan.

Chaplain John Routzahn has been a chaplain endorsed by the Presbyterian Church in America since 1992. Among his many assignments, he has been deployed to Honduras, Korea, Egypt, Kuwait, the Netherlands, Iraq and Afghanistan. He and his wife, Cheryl, have a daughter, Meghan.

In response to Chaplain Lawhorn's letter, Chaplain Routzahn had this to say: "I am moved to tears at the goodness of God, and in particular the goodness of Him in your life . . . . I have a great sense of rejoicing right now . . . . You have warmed my heart by and with God's grace and love."

18

A SONG OF PRAYER

CHAPLAIN LORRAINE POTTER

MAJOR GENERAL, U.S. AIR FORCE, RETIRED

Throughout my military career, I was privileged to speak at many National Prayer Breakfast services around the country and overseas.

One time, following one of these programs at an Air Force base on the East Coast, a young woman came up to me and asked if she could "sing me a prayer."

Several years earlier, this young U.S. servicewoman told me, she was stationed at Lakenheath Royal Air Force Base in England and attended a National Prayer Breakfast there. She went that day for one purpose only—to fulfill a promise she had made to a friend. In reality, she intended it to be the last thing she ever did. She was planning to take her own life.

I was Command Chaplain in Europe at the time, and I spoke at that breakfast. I talked about how we can be "God with skin on."

I began with a story about a child whose bedtime has come, but who is afraid to go to sleep. She begs a drink of water from her mother, a trip to the bathroom, another bedtime story. The child's mother soothes the child, reminds her that she's already had everything she's asking for. She tells her child that she'll leave a light on in the hallway, but that she has everything she needs to go to sleep.

"Remember, dear," she finishes. "God is with you all the time, and God will never let anything harm you."

Even so, the child isn't satisfied.

"But, mommy," she protests. "I need God with skin on!"

That's what we all need. We need to be the outward embodiment of God in each other's lives, to show each other the grace, the mercy, the peace, the forgiveness of God. It's not a special calling for chaplains or for pastors; it's a calling for every one of us. It's a message I gave that day, as I did many other times, because it is a message we all need to hear.

I did not meet this young woman that day, but two years later, here she was in front of me, recalling what was going on in her mind at that first prayer breakfast.

That morning in England, she said, my message touched her heart and soothed her troubled mind. Although she didn't say anything to me then, she went home determined to work through her despair and difficult situations.

"You gave me the courage to believe that I could handle what I was facing," she said. Heartened and hopeful, she abandoned her plan to kill herself.

Yet, all was not well. Now, two years later, this young woman said, she was again struggling with feelings of depression and doubt. So, when she saw that I was to speak at her Air Force base, she knew she had to come. "God sent you here just for me," she said.

"I am experiencing a time of despair," she admitted to me. "But this time I want to sing a prayer of hope and gratitude."

Now, I can't carry a tune in a tin bucket, so I am blessed by anyone who can sing. Right where we were, we stood facing each other, our hands clasped, tears coming down our cheeks as she sang. She sang an old gospel song, praising God for his faithfulness, for his presence in times of trouble. With her story and her song, she ministered as much to me as I did to her. Yes, God does work in wonderful ways, using all of us as "God with skin on."

Chaplain Lorraine Potter is an ordained American Baptist minister. Commissioned in 1973, she became the first female chaplain in the U.S. Air Force. She was the first woman chaplain of all branches of military service to be promoted to colonel, brigadier general and major general. She served at every installation and command level in the Department of Defense and retired in 2004 as Chief of the Air Force Chaplain Service. She and her husband, Chaplain Robert Saunders, a retired Army Colonel, live in San Antonio, Texas.

19

LOOKING INTO HELL

CHAPLAIN LAURENCE BAZER

LIEUTENANT COLONEL, MASSACHUSETTS ARMY
NATIONAL GUARD

CHAPLAIN BRAD HOFFMAN

COMMANDER, U.S. NAVY RESERVE

The Twin Towers: Chaplain Bazer

When the Twin Towers fell on September 11, I was called up for duty
with my National Guard unit. I kissed my family goodbye and told
them I wasn't sure when I'd be home.

I lived on Long Island then, and so it took me several hours to make
my way into the city. Traffic was piled up on the Long Island Express-
way, and it was slow going until the point at which state police were
letting only emergency personnel vehicles through.

I crossed into Queens and from there saw the Manhattan skyline.
An enormous black and grey cloud of smoke rose up from the hori-
zon in the area of the Twin Towers. Finally, I made it into the city
and parked on the East Side, at a firehouse along the East River. From
there, I began walking.

By the time I got to the Wall Street area, it was about 12:30 or 1 o'clock. All around me, it looked as if people had just vanished. They had abandoned their belongings as they ran—at a Starbucks I saw half-filled coffee cups and scattered newspaper pages. Everything in sight was covered in grey soot. I passed an abandoned fruit and vegetable cart, the produce on the side facing the Towers covered in soot. To me, it looked like the pictures you see of Hiroshima.

I tried to get my bearings, to decide which way to walk. In New York, you'd use the Towers as a guide, almost as a compass, so instinctively I looked up. They weren't there. It was a shocking realization. As I got closer to the site, the scene was chaotic. People were running away, rescue workers were everywhere.

When I was a block away from Ground Zero, I was met with an all-encompassing cloud of billowing black smoke and soot. I turned and looked north, and was startled to see beautifully clear, blue skies. Then I looked back down a street leading directly to the World Trade Center. Where its buildings were supposed to be, I saw only blackness surrounded by a ring of angry fire. It was like looking into hell.

I worked at Ground Zero for many days, usually on the night shift, ministering to our soldiers, law enforcement personnel and rescue workers. One night while on duty—it was the Saturday after the attack following the conclusion of my Sabbath—I went up to the edge of the blast site, near where the South Tower had been. Along the edges of the pile of rubble I saw orange Xs marking the spots where fallen heroes and victims might be found. I stood on the curb and looked down. The whole building had just collapsed into a deep pit. The ruins smoked and smoldered into the dark night.

As I stood there, sobered by the sight of such massive destruction, a firefighter came up alongside me. From his helmet, I could tell he was a senior firefighter, perhaps a captain.

"Did you lose anyone from your station?" I asked him.

He replied that all of his firefighters were safe, but said he had known ten of the 343 firefighters who had lost their lives that day.

"Would you say a prayer for them?" he asked.

I told the firefighter I was Jewish—I thought I needed to tell him—and he said that was fine with him. And, so, in the incredible darkness of that place, I prayed that God would remember all those who had fallen, that He would give strength to the families who had lost loved ones, and that we would persevere and be strong as a nation as we fought the darkness with light.

We both had tears in our eyes as we prayed. We no longer felt alone; we felt the comfort that God provides by bringing people together. We experienced God's presence in that dark place. I believe this knowledge of divine presence is what people truly seek in times of great need.

The Pentagon: Chaplain Hoffman

On the morning of September 11, I was teaching a class at Philadelphia University. A student came into the classroom and said that a plane had hit the World Trade Center. We all just assumed it was a terrible accident of some sort. But then the second plane hit, the third hit the Pentagon and a fourth crashed in a Pennsylvania field. That's when I thought to myself: *We're at war!*

There was nothing we could do, so I went on with the class. When we had finished, I drove to my mother's house in Center City

Philadelphia. Here, in the middle of a city that's always busy, I saw the strangest sight: There were virtually no cars on the street. It was deserted.

I was engaged to be married at the time, so when I talked to my fiancé, who is now my wife, I assured her that I was in no danger. "I'm an inactive Reservist," I told her. "There's no chance I'll be called up."

Nevertheless, at 7 o'clock that night, I got a call from the Chief of Chaplains Office, asking if I were willing to serve.

"I'll do whatever you want me to do," I said. They sent me to the Pentagon.

The drive to Washington was eerie. Nobody was on the highway; I could have gone 200 miles an hour if I had wanted to. I got to the friend's house where I was staying in no time at all.

When I arrived at the Pentagon at about midnight, I was stunned. There was a huge, gaping hole in the side of the building. Everything was charred from the fire and heat of the plane's impact. It was odd, but I remember looking up and seeing a small blinking light on the third floor of the building. It was a computer screen, still powered up and working.

The site was chaotic. The smell of death was in the air, and it was overpowering. We were given gas masks to wear as we worked, but that only muted the smell. Rescuers were hard at work all around me, streaming in and out of the Pentagon.

One group of rescuers was preparing to go into the building, but they stopped when they saw me.

"Will you pray for us?" they asked.

Of course, I said I would. But they wanted even more.

"We're not going in without a chaplain," they said. They believed that God's hand of protection would be on them if a chaplain were present with them.

At the time, I was scheduled to conduct High Holy Day services at the site. I contacted the chaplain command post and waited with the firefighters until another chaplain arrived to accompany them in. I could see a sense of calm and reassurance settle over the firefighters as they proceeded into the Pentagon.

I worked at the Pentagon in 12-hour shifts starting that night. In that time, I saw some of the most compassionate, most professional work that I've ever seen in military service. I have a special respect for those working in mortuary affairs who had the grim task of retrieving and identifying the bodies of people who had died. Whenever remains were found, everyone observed a moment of respectful silence, and many times I was asked to say a prayer.

As chaplains, we help people deal with extreme emotions. In the days after the attack, we consoled families who were overcome with the grief of losing loved ones. When, in anger, people called for the deaths of others to atone for the deed, we focused attention on the fact that the attackers did not represent an entire religion or an entire nation. For people who were afraid, people who didn't know the whereabouts of their friends and family, we represented the reassuring presence of God.

September 11 was a watershed event for our country, like World War II was for an earlier generation. Everything changed on that day. The attacks had an effect on our national psyche that will last for decades. The lessons we learned that day may not stay with us forever, but for the moment we were united. There were no Democrats, no Republicans, no Independents. Military rank meant nothing. It was an *esprit de corps* brought on by the most extreme circumstances. It was a privilege to serve on that day.

Chaplain Laurence Bazer has been an Army chaplain endorsed by the Jewish Chaplains Council for 21 years, serving in the Army National Guard for both Massachusetts and New York. Rabbi Bazer is the Joint Forces State Chaplain for the Massachusetts Army National Guard, the first Jewish chaplain to serve in this capacity for the state, and he is a chaplain for the Boston office of the FBI. Rabbi Bazer is a full-time congregational rabbi for Temple Beth Sholom in Framingham, Massachusetts. When he was called up on 9/11, he was a rabbi for a congregation on Long Island. He and his wife, Leslie, have two children, Oren and Eliana.

Chaplain Brad Hoffman is a Navy Reserve chaplain endorsed by the Jewish Chaplains Council who has been on active duty since 1996. Prior to that, Rabbi Hoffman served for six years on active duty with the Navy. In addition to being called up on 9/11, he was deployed to Iraq in 2006. He is an adjunct faculty member at St. Joseph's University in Philadelphia, where he teaches an Introduction to Judaism course. He and his wife, Diane, have two children, Layten and Logan.

20

A SINGLE DEATH

CHAPLAIN STAN GILES
LIEUTENANT COLONEL,
TENNESSEE AIR NATIONAL GUARD

The dictator Joseph Stalin infamously said, *"A single death is a tragedy; a million deaths is a statistic."* It is a chilling statement, but one that aptly sums up the difficulty of comprehending the horror of war.

I grew up in a military home and lived in Germany in the early 1960s. Having no television, we often went to the base theater on Fridays and watched movies. My favorites were the World War II films, the ones you see on cable channels now.

Afterwards, my friends and I would reenact the battle scenes in fields outside our quaint German village. Using rocks for grenades and whatever toy guns we could scrounge, we played war. Sometimes we fought the Japanese, but mostly we fought the Germans—it was convenient. Casualties were common, but we all lived to fight another day. For us, war was a game.

In the summer of 1963, when I was eight years old, our family went on a camping trip through southern Europe. This was the era of

Europe-on-five-dollars-a-day, so the six of us plus our grandmother
squeezed into a '55 Buick and took off.

One morning, while winding our way through the hills south of Rome,
we made an impromptu stop at the World War II Sicily–Rome American
Cemetery. I was numb to the significance of the site but grateful for the
reprieve from sitting. We spilled out of the car and went exploring.

It was a clear summer morning and the heavy scent of newly mown
grass hung thick in the air. I remember a fountain and a shallow
memorial pool, which naturally captivated my attention. Beyond
the pool was a field of memorial crosses, the name of a fallen soldier
engraved on each one, nearly 8,000 of them in all.

The crosses were arranged in gentle arcs on broad green lawns
beneath rows of Roman pines. I was mesmerized by the sight of
them. Regardless of where I stood, they were aligned in perfect order,
standing as though called to attention.

When I caught up with my family, my mother was crying
softly. Concerned, I asked my father what was wrong. He was an Air
Force sergeant and fit the profile well—he wasn't prone to coddling
kids. But that morning, with all the gentleness of Mr. Rogers, he put
his arm around me and quietly explained that these 8,000 men had
died in "The War," the one that I saw re-created in the movies, the one
that I played at. That reality made my mother sad, he said.

It was at that moment in the hills of Italy that I made the con-
nection between war and death. Until then it was just a game
played between friends, with the only casualties scraped elbows
and knees. But that morning I learned that war brought death
and sadness.

Many years later, after I had grown up and married, I learned the very same lesson. But this time, it was the lesson of a single death.

In the basement family room of the Iowa farmhouse my wife grew up in is a collage of family photos. On one wall are six groupings of photographs corresponding to the six children born to Harold and Faye Kahlstorf. There are three photos each of my wife and her five brothers, eighteen pictures in all.

The arrangement for four of them is identical: a childhood picture, a high school graduation picture and a wedding picture. But there are two exceptions: Jeffrey, who died as a boy in a farm accident, and Keith, who was killed in Vietnam.

In lieu of a wedding picture, my wife's family has displayed Keith's official Marine photo. Tucked inside the frame is a faded snapshot taken in Vietnam. It's a candid shot of him in his olive drab fatigues. He is sitting on the wall of a Buddhist temple, his M-16 rifle next to him. Unlike in his official photo, Keith is grinning slightly. You can imagine a scoffing, "Hey, man, what are you doing?" in his expression.

Soon afterwards, Keith was killed in a mortar attack. He was just 20 years old.

My wife Sandi tells of the sad day when she was called out of class to report to the principal's office. Her peers teased her at this uncommon invitation and her confusion grew when she saw her father waiting for her in the hall. When she stepped out of the classroom, he exclaimed, "They got him! They got Keith!"

The rural community embraced my wife's family and mourned the loss of one of their own. The crowd at the funeral was huge, as many of his peers made the pilgrimage home. At the graveside service, a minister and a chaplain offered prayers, and sharply dressed Marines folded a flag and fired a 21-gun salute with absolute precision. A bugler played taps.

Then life did what it always does; it moved on.

Years ago when I married into the family, I heard little about Keith. In time, I grew curious about this brother-in-law I never knew.

Physically he was about my size, perhaps a bit taller, and we shared the same shoe size. I know that because my mother-in-law gave his service boots to me. I used them mostly for hunting. Looking back I regret that, for, while the usage was practical, it now seems a bit irreverent. But when I was sitting quietly in a deer blind, I did think about Keith.

Keith Kahlstorf grew up on a farm—perhaps the last of a generation to live on a modest, but adequately sized farm. He worked hard at chores but in between he managed a social life centered on high school and sports. He was a decent student and a good wrestler, a state champion in his weight class. He was a dutiful son, a helpful big brother to his sister, and a good Marine. He dreamed of finishing college and becoming a teacher and wrestling coach. But the fatal combination of the draft and a mortar shell put an end to that dream.

In its June 27, 1969 issue, *Life* magazine published a pictorial collection of every soldier who had died in Vietnam during the last week of May. That happened to be the week Keith was killed—May 25, 1969.

So there on page 27 is Keith's Marine photo along with a caption giving his name, age and home town. In all, 242 names were printed in the magazine—242 body bags were needed that week, 242 funerals were held—"average for any seven-day period during that stage of the war," the writer pointed out.

When you study war, casualties are statistics; maybe not *mere* statistics, but statistics nevertheless. It is almost impossible to put your emotional arms around thousands of war dead. But when you are connected with a single casualty, war becomes tragic.

Today, when my wife and I visit her family, I make it a point to go downstairs and ponder the pictures. I look at them all, but I always pause in front of the good-looking, steely-eyed young Marine. I guess it is my way of memorializing his sacrifice.

Forty years ago, Keith Kahlstorf was a young man with a lifetime ahead of him; now he is a fading memory. There is a whole nation of people who did not know him, but there remain a few people who think of him, who miss him, every day. And it's because of thousands of stories like his—stories of a single tragedy—that we can understand the sacrifice he and other soldiers, sailors, airmen and Marines have made on our behalf.

Chaplain Stan Giles is a chaplain on active duty with the Tennessee Air National Guard stationed in Knoxville. He was a parish pastor for many years, serving in the Evangelical Free Church. He has deployed to both Iraq and Afghanistan and is currently on active duty. Chaplain Giles is a frequent guest columnist for the Knoxville News Sentinel. *He and his wife, Sandi, have two children, Scott and Shannon.*

21

I'm Not Going Back There

CHAPLAIN JOHN GROTH

LIEUTENANT COLONEL,

U.S. AIR FORCE RESERVE, RETIRED

I was called to the break room of the mortuary at Dover Air Force Base one day. "Chaplain, you've got to talk to an airman. She's having a tough time," my chaplain's assistant said.

At Dover, it was my job to minister to those who processed the remains of our servicemen and women who have been killed overseas. It is mostly reservists who do this job. Quickly, I made my way down the hall and into the break room.

A small group huddled around the airman. They looked uncomfortable and parted gratefully when I arrived. The airman was seated at a table, crying. Not sobbing, or heaving, not making any noise at all. Tears were just rolling down her cheeks. I pulled up a chair.

I thought for a second about what to say. I didn't want to ask her how she was doing. When you do that, people always say, "I'm okay, Chaplain." It's just an ingrained response. You never get to the heart of the matter with that question. I took a different approach.

"It's tough back there, isn't it?" I said to her.

The airman didn't look at me. She kept looking down.

"Yeah, it's really hard," she said. "And I'm not going back there."

"Is this your first time?" I asked.

"I am not going back there," she answered, tears still streaming down her face.

No matter what I asked, that was her answer.

"You're not from this base, are you?" I asked.

"No, I'm not," she said. "And I'm not going back there."

"What base are you from?" I asked.

She told me the name of the base. "And I'm not going back there," she added.

"I see you're a reservist," I said. "Tell me. What do you do in your civilian life?"

"I'm a hairdresser," she said. "And I'm not going back there."

"Airman," I said. "I really need for you to look me in the eye for a minute. I have to ask you something."

Reluctantly, she lifted her eyes to mine.

"You've told me you're a hairdresser," I said. She answered, "Yes, and I am not going back there."

I pointed to my head, with its severe Air Force haircut imposed on my balding scalp.

"So, do you have any suggestions for what to do with this?" I asked her.

The airman hesitated for a second, staring at me. Then, incredibly, she started to laugh. And then it was like a dam broke and all her emotions came gushing out. She was laughing, and then sobbing, and then laughing and sobbing at the same time. Finally, she looked up at me again.

"Chaplain, did I ever need that!" she said, gasping and wiping her eyes. "And, I am *not* going back there."

"Airman," I replied. "You don't have to go back there."

On my way to the break room, I had stopped by the First Sergeant's office and gotten his permission for her to be reassigned to the administrative section. She really didn't have to go back there. Greatly relieved, she thanked me for arranging her new duties.

The next day, I came into the break room and was astonished to see the airman there, gowned up in protective gear. She was dressed for the mortuary, not administrative work.

"Chaplain, I've thought about it," she said. "And I'm not going to let this defeat me. I've been working for two hours and I'm okay. I can do this!"

The airman had a huge smile on her face. That positive attitude stayed with her for the next five days as she processed the remains of our fallen heroes, preparing them to be sent home to their families for burial.

Six or seven months later, I was called to Dover for another incident. When I arrived, I headed for the lodging desk to get my room for the week. Just then, this same airman came in. She was dressed in civilian clothes and leading a group of three young airmen. She saw me at the desk and quickly came over to greet me.

"Chaplain, I'm a sergeant now. I got promoted," she said. "I've been brought in to teach these young reservists the job."

As she spoke, she had the same huge smile that I remembered from the break room all those months ago.

Almost to a person, everyone who works at the mortuary will tell you that it's the hardest tour they've ever done, but also the best tour they've done. They understand the importance of their mission and they are fiercely proud of their work. Engraved over the entryway to the mortuary are three words: Dignity, Honor, Respect. At Dover, they abide by these words as they serve their fellow airmen, Marines, soldiers and sailors.

Chaplain John Groth retired in 2009 as Wing Chaplain for the U.S. Air Force Reserve after serving for more than 21 years. Endorsed by the Presbyterian Church (USA), he ministered for eight years to those processing the remains of fallen servicemen and women at Dover Air Force Base. Today, he works with the men's ministry PriorityOne Foundation. He and his wife, Ranelle, have three children, Erin, John and Shannon.

22

THANK YOU, MERCY!

CHAPLAIN JOHN OWEN

COMMANDER, U.S. NAVY

Iqbal was a handsome Indonesian boy. He was about eight or nine years old, all jet black hair and big, dark eyes. But when I first saw Iqbal, he was in a coma, lying motionless in a hospital bed.

When the tsunami of December 2004 devastated Southeast Asia, I was assigned as chaplain to a medical disaster team aboard the hospital ship USNS *Mercy*. We were sent to aid ongoing U.S. relief efforts in the area.

The ship was huge—12 operating rooms, an 80-bed intensive care unit and 1,000 hospital beds—and it was staffed by both Navy and civilian medical personnel. We headed out of San Diego harbor a few days after receiving word of our mission. We arrived at Banda Aceh, a city at the northern tip of the Indonesian island of Sumatra, a little over a month after the tsunami.

In the dozen or so countries ravaged by the tsunami, more than 226,000 people had been killed. Aceh Province was perhaps the hardest hit. The earthquake that set off the tsunami had struck about 155 miles south of the province. Some villages along the coast lost more

than half of their inhabitants. Many thousands more were injured
and hundreds of thousands left homeless.

We anchored off the coast and began sending teams in to the local
hospital. The hospital was a complex of one- and two-story buildings.
Water had entirely flooded the buildings up to the second story; the
tsunami had killed everyone on the first floor. The hospital was left
with no medical infrastructure. We were there to offer *Mercy*'s extraordinary medical care and to get the hospital up and running again. We
joined military medical teams from around the globe—China, Spain,
Germany, New Zealand, Australia.

At first, it was not easy going. The Indonesian government was
ambivalent about us being there. The province had been fighting low-
level separatist battles with the government. The local people, being
primarily Muslim and not sure of who they could trust, were understandably wary of Westerners.

Word got around pretty quickly, though, that we were there just to
treat sick people, and the locals accepted our care more readily. We
began transporting people to the ship by helicopter.

We had been there only a day or two when we brought Iqbal
aboard. He was a very sick little boy, our first critically ill patient.

Iqbal was accompanied by his young uncle. Through an interpreter,
we learned that rescuers had found Iqbal two or three days after the
tsunami, floating on a piece of debris. He was the only survivor of his
immediate family—Iqbal's mother and father and his siblings had all
been washed out to sea and drowned. He was an orphan.

Before his rescue, Iqbal had taken in a large amount of seawater. As
you can imagine, the salt water was filled with mud and bacteria, all

manner of nasty stuff. He was among the first patients we encountered with a pneumonia-like condition that later was called "tsunami lung."

Infections had set in and were ravaging Iqbal's body. The infections had spread through his bloodstream and into his brain. The doctors worked tirelessly on Iqbal, but he remained in a coma.

One night, I went down to the ICU to check on Iqbal. He was hooked up to a ventilator and things did not look good. Doctors there told me that this night was going to determine the boy's fate—that the crisis was going to break one way or the other.

"We'll see what the night brings," one doctor said to me.

The urgency of the situation pressed on my heart. I went to Iqbal's bedside and sat down. I took his small hand in mine. In that moment, I was overcome with emotion.

I am the one God has brought here for this moment, I thought. *There is no place I belong more than right here, right now.*

To this day, I'm not sure exactly what happened, but at that moment I was overtaken with an image of Iqbal's parents looking down on him. They could not be there with their little boy, but I realized that I could be. It was for them, as much as for him, that I felt God had called me to be at Iqbal's side.

I stroked Iqbal's head and prayed for him. Finally, there was nothing to do but leave him in God's hands.

First thing the next morning, I went down to the ICU to check on Iqbal, not knowing what I would find. When I arrived, the medical staff was all smiles. Iqbal had survived the night!

Not only did he survive, but soon his coma lifted. Within a few days, doctors removed the ventilator and Iqbal began to breathe on his own. Gradually he became stronger. He started to get around with a wheelchair, and eventually he walked a little. He was shy, and he didn't speak any English, but he smiled all the time.

The crew gave him the run of the ship. We took turns wheeling him up on deck so he could enjoy the sunshine. The crew showed him all of the ship's operations. He liked to be on the flight deck, sitting in the chair reserved for the Air Boss—the officer who directed helicopters between ship and shore. He'd sit in the big chair, giant binoculars in hand, enjoying the hum of activity around him. The ship's barber came up one day to his hospital bed to give him a haircut. I'm not sure who enjoyed that more, the barber or the boy.

Incredibly, six weeks after he came aboard, Iqbal was ready to leave the hospital. I was privileged to accompany him ashore, his wheelchair loaded down with stuffed animals, sunglasses, baseball caps and other gifts from the crew. As we made our way through the ship, everyone stopped what they were doing to say goodbye to this smiling little boy who had burrowed his way into our hearts.

I took a photo of Iqbal on one of his last days aboard ship. In it, he is lying in bed, his head propped up on a pillow, and he's clutching a stuffed lion. His smile is a mile wide. His uncle, standing beside Iqbal's bed, grins in sheer happiness, too. On his white t-shirt he has written in red marker, in English: "Mercy! Thank you all!"

For everyone aboard the ship, Iqbal's recovery was a symbol of what we were there for. This gentle and smiling boy lifted our spirits. His uncle was deeply grateful for the care we had given Iqbal. In fact, every person we treated was gracious and so very thankful for our help, even those for whom we could do nothing except make them more comfortable. I learned a lot about gratitude from the Indonesian people.

Most precious to me, though, was that moment beside Iqbal's bed. It was very powerful, a profound moment. It blessed me with a strong sense of the holiness of our mission. I've had moments of insight in my life, but nothing that compares to this clear message from God, this whisper that was audible only to me. It was a moment of grace.

Chaplain John Owen is an ordained Presbyterian minister. He was a helicopter pilot for the Coast Guard for nearly ten years before becoming a pastor and subsequently a Navy chaplain. In addition to his time aboard the Mercy, he has served with the Marines and with Navy ships, including deployment to the Western Pacific and Persian Gulf for Operation Enduring Freedom. In 2007, while serving at the United States Naval Academy, he was appointed chaplain of the football team that season. He wrote a book about his experience, titled Into the Fire *(iUniverse, 2008). He is currently assigned as command chaplain aboard USS Enterprise (CVN 65). He and his wife, Shelly, have two daughters, Courtney and Claire.*

23

I'LL DO ANYTHING

CHAPLAIN BEVERLY BARNETT

LIEUTENANT COLONEL, U.S. AIR FORCE, RETIRED

I can do everything through him who gives me strength.

PHILIPPIANS 4:13

One day while serving as chaplain for the hospital at Ellsworth Air Force Base in South Dakota, I opened my office door to find Bill, the dispensary's non-commissioned officer in charge. When he walked in, he looked like he had lost his last friend.

As Bill sat down with me, he blurted out that he had never been to a church before, had never talked with a minister or with a chaplain before. I nodded and tried to put him at ease. Then, he told me the sad story of his life.

Bill admitted that he was a problem drinker and probably an alcoholic. He stashed alcohol in hidden places around the dispensary so he could drink throughout the day. His drinking, not surprisingly, was becoming a liability on the job.

But, worst of all, his drinking had cost him his wife and family. When he drank, Bill was a cruel man, given to physical violence. Twice, his wife had taken their children and gone back to her home in a southern state. Each time, after he had sobered up, he followed her and made convincing promises that he wouldn't drink again if she returned. Both times, she returned, but each time it wasn't long before he was back to the bottle.

Finally, his wife left him for good. She left a note. "This is the last time, Bill," she wrote. "We're never coming back. Do not come and see us ever again."

Bill realized the resolve of her tone and the finality of her decision. For a few days, he drowned his grief in yet more alcohol. When he finally sobered up, he ended up in my office.

"Can you help me, Chaplain?" he cried out in desperation. "I love my wife and family and I want them back."

My heart went out to Bill.

"Bill," I said to him, "I may have an answer for you, but it will depend on how sincere you are."

"Chaplain, I'll do anything to bring my family back," he said.

With that, I told Bill that Christ could forgive his sins and help him overcome his destructive habit. He had never heard this message before, but he took it to heart readily. Soon we were both on our knees.

I began to pray first and then urged Bill to say the words of a prayer of salvation after me. I didn't get very far with the prayer I had in mind. Bill launched into his own prayer, his voice rising in anxious crescendo, like a drowning man yelling for help.

Bill told God what a great sinner he had been and pleaded for forgiveness. He asked God to come into his life and deliver him from his addiction to alcohol. After this prayer, he continued with a more subdued prayer, giving thanks to God for his mercy to him. He asked God to put it in his wife's heart to forgive him, too.

As we rose from our knees, what a changed man stood before me! The smile on his face reflected a heart of peace.

After that day, Bill stopped in to see me every few days. About a month later, however, I realized I hadn't seen him in a few days, and I became worried. Had Bill gone back to drinking?

A few days later, Bill rushed into my office. Without any preliminaries, he blurted out, "Chaplain, let me tell you what happened!" I steeled myself for the worst.

"This past weekend I went into Rapid City with some of my buddies," he said. "We stopped at a bar, one of my favorite bars that I used to frequent. I had no desire to drink, and my friends knew that I had sworn off alcohol.

"But as I watched my friends drink, I wondered what would happen if I took a drink—curiosity, you know—so I ordered a beer and began to drink."

My heart sank when I heard this. But Bill wasn't finished.

"Chaplain, after the first swallow of beer, I got so sick I threw up!" he said triumphantly.

With a sigh of relief, I told Bill that his experiment, while a success, was unwise. In my experience, while God will sometimes totally deliver a person from an addiction—and it looks like this was true in Bill's case—other times He will grant only the strength to resist the temptation. The day may come, I warned him, that you will reject that strength, and instead give in to the temptation. Bill agreed with me that he would not experiment in this way again.

Some months later, Bill was reassigned to a base in Texas. He came to see me before he left. He said he planned to stop and visit his wife and family en route to his new assignment.

"I'm not going to ask her to come with me," he said. "I'm hoping she will see that I have changed and will want to join me again."

Some weeks later, I received a letter from Bill. He was ecstatic—his wife and children had joined him! They were happy, he said, and looking for a church home. Later, he wrote again to say that he and his family were active in an Assemblies of God church and helping church leaders start a sister church. He was holding fast to his faith. The Lord is faithful and good.

Chaplain Beverly Barnett retired as an Air Force chaplain in 1981 after serving in the military for 28 years as a Wesleyan chaplain endorsed by the Methodist Commission on Chaplains. Following his retirement, he served on the pastoral staff of two churches as an ordained Presbyterian Church of America minister. Chaplain Barnett and his wife, Margie, have two adult children, Mark and Deanne, and six grandsons. He has written a book about his experiences as a chaplain titled For God and Country: Memoirs of a Military Chaplain *(Xulon Press, 2008), from which "I'll Do Anything" is excerpted and adapted with permission.*

24

A Chaplain's Cross

Chaplain Dallas Little
Captain, U.S. Air Force

My father, Chester Vesteen Little, has always been a source of great inspiration to me and a wonderful model of a Christian father and an American patriot.

My dad was a hard worker—he was at various times a bricklayer, an auto mechanic and a prison guard. He and my mother embodied honesty and earnestness in their personal lives and work ethic. They raised my twin sister and me with great faithfulness. They had become parents when they were almost 40, so for us it was almost like being raised by grandparents. The home my parents created was inviting and hospitable. It became a refuge for many of our friends who came from tough home situations.

I had the privilege as a teenager of attending my dad's retirement party at the Alabama prison where he'd worked the night shift. Some of the prisoners he was close to were allowed to attend, and they formed a barbershop quartet to sing for him. It was an incredible sight—some of the guys actually cried as they said their good-byes. It's an image I cling to even today, especially when I'm in deployed situations. I try to bring something positive to my work, the way my dad ministered in a place I can't even imagine going to every day.

Dad's example had a tremendous impact on my decision to become a chaplain. He had been in the Air Force during the Korean War, stationed on Guam maintaining a B-50 bomber. He worked on the same aircraft for his entire wartime deployment, fixing the engine and electrical systems, refueling it, maintaining the hydraulics. He had a photo of the plane enlarged and framed for me shortly before I entered the Air Force. It always hangs in my chapel office.

In addition to his prison job, my dad was deputized as an adjunct deputy sheriff and was always interested in law enforcement. Inspired by him, I went to college to major in forensic science. I had an ROTC scholarship and wanted to become an Army CID agent. My dad even took me to an FBI recruiting session at one point, encouraging me in my pursuits.

But while at college, I felt a powerful and unexpected call to the ministry. I switched my educational emphasis and prepared instead for seminary. The first church I pastored was in Fort Walton Beach, Florida. It was situated between two Air Force bases, and many church members were active duty military, retired military and contractors for these bases. I was surrounded by Air Force blue. My interest in the military grew, and in 2001, I applied to the Air Force Chaplain Corps.

The church honored my entrance into the military chaplaincy by conducting a worship service of consecration. It was a very moving experience for me. The music director performed an original piece of music for the occasion. One dear woman presented me with the

World War II communion kit her father, an Army chaplain, had used to minister to wounded soldiers. As I knelt at the altar after taking the Officers' Oath, my mother and my wife pinned the military rank insignia on the shoulder epaulets of my service dress uniform, which I was wearing for the first time. My father capped off the ceremony by pinning the Chaplain's Cross on my jacket, right above my heart.

It was especially fitting for my father to pin the cross on my uniform. Dad always wore a religious emblem on the lapel of his suit or sport coat. It was a ubiquitous and endearing personal signature. He had a huge array of Christian symbols—crosses, the Ichthus, doves of peace. He finished his long military career as a Seabee in the Navy Reserves and when he'd return from drill weekends and his annual training, he'd bring home military emblems and pins for me. I remember wearing shiny Navy flight wings to church on my child-sized jacket, proudly walking beside Dad, wearing his own glittering lapel pins.

Dad passed away seven years ago, at the age of 71, after a terrible struggle with cancer. I'd been in the military only a year when he became ill and was fortunate to be stationed near his home at Keesler Air Force Base in Biloxi, Mississipi. I was able to spend a lot of time with him as the cancer worsened. Dad's slow decline and death was one of the most traumatic things I've ever been through, something I still grieve. Although it was hard for me, I agreed to speak at his funeral and to preside over the military ceremony accompanying the interment of his coffin.

As we were making arrangements for my father's funeral, my mom asked my opinion on the clothes he should be buried in. I looked at the suit she'd selected and something didn't seem right to me. Then I noticed it—the jacket's lapel was bare. I knew immediately what I wanted to do. I took out my dress uniform and unpinned my Chaplain's Cross—the very same cross my dad had pinned on me a few years before—and I affixed it to his lapel.

It comforted me greatly to perform that small act of blessing for my father. I often reflect on that moment when I'm suiting up. As I slip on my service dress coat, I look at the emblem of faith on my lapel and remember not only my sustaining Redeemer, but the strength and simple faith of the father who first pinned a Chaplain's Cross on me.

Chaplain Dallas Little is endorsed as an Air Force chaplain by the United Methodist Church and was a civilian pastor for five years in Florida before entering the military. Rev. Dr. Little was one of the first Air Force chaplains to enter Iraq during Operation Iraqi Freedom and is currently helping to develop new techniques for ministering to service members suffering from post-traumatic stress disorder. He is married to his high school sweetheart, Janice, and they are the parents of two children, Trevor and Zoe.

25

A MOTHER'S PHOTO

CHAPLAIN RICHARD MARTIN

COLONEL, U.S. ARMY, RETIRED

I arrived at the little white Methodist church with about an hour to spare. I was there to conduct the funeral of a soldier killed in combat in Vietnam the spring of 1969. At the time, I was stationed at Fort Leavenworth, Kansas. The base chaplains took part in a rotation when a chaplain was needed for a military funeral service. I had been assigned to take this young man's service. His family lived a few hours away in a small town in southern Iowa.

I walked into the church along with the honor guard that had traveled with me—a firing party, a bugler and a flag-folding unit—maybe eight of us in all. The pastor met us at the door and suggested we might like to meet with the family before the service. We followed him through the church to the fellowship hall in back.

I always like to say something personal about the soldier whose life I'm honoring, so I was eager to meet with his mother and father. We talked for a while, and then I turned away to greet other members of the family. While I was shaking hands and talking, however, I began to get an odd sensation of being watched. You know how uncomfortable that can make you feel.

The feeling followed me as I made my way around the room. With a start, I realized that I was indeed being watched. The parents of the young soldier were staring at me, staring hard. They were so intent it was making me really uneasy. Finally, the mother nudged her husband, and I heard her exclaim, "I think that's him!"

Out of the corner of my eye, I watched as she reached into her purse and pulled something out. It looked like a newspaper article. She rushed over to me and pointed to it. "Is that you?" she asked.

In the mother's hands was a four-month-old photo clipped from an Army newspaper. The photo showed a semicircle of soldiers attending a makeshift worship service in the middle of a Vietnam jungle. The mother was pointing to the chaplain conducting the service.

That chaplain was indeed me.

Before arriving at Fort Leavenworth, I had been assigned to the 25th Infantry Division for a year-long tour of duty in Vietnam. We were stationed about 40 miles north of Saigon at Cu Chi. I roved around from unit to unit, hitching a ride on any helicopter going my way. Wherever I went, I conducted Protestant services. I usually made an announcement about the service in the evening chow line.

It wasn't safe anywhere, so for the services we would surround ourselves with two or three vehicles within the temporary base camp. The guys would all be in their combat gear, flak vests and helmets. They'd lay their weapons on the ground beside them. It was sort of like setting up our own protective perimeter there.

I would unpack my chaplain kit, which was a container about the size of a backpack that contained a cross, a chalice, Communion elements, song sheets and a small stand for a Bible. The soldiers had their duties to perform, so I kept the service short, no longer than 15 or 20 minutes, but we sang hymns, and I would give a brief homily and allow time for silent prayer and reflection. I'd conclude by offering Communion to the soldiers who wanted it. Most did.

That day, the day the photo was taken, the driver of an armored personnel carrier (APC) offered his track for the altar. An armored personnel carrier has a heavy metal plate at the front that slopes back and protects soldiers from the impact of an explosion. But it also folds down to make a perfect altar.

The driver of the APC helped me set up the makeshift altar. I knew this soldier well, having talked to him many times while visiting his unit. I enjoyed his company. He was a sharp young man, with a kind of bubbly personality, an all-American kind of kid. He came to every service I conducted for this unit.

He was also in the photo his grieving mother held out to me.

The young man had mailed the clipping home to his parents. He had drawn an arrow pointing to one of the soldiers and written in the margin, "This is me!" She had carried it in her purse from the day they had received it.

Now, standing in front of me, the mother of this young man gasped as she realized I had known her son. It was like the floodgates had opened! She reached out and grabbed me and hugged me tight. She cried as we embraced.

In that moment, I scrapped what I had planned to say at this young man's funeral service. Instead, as I looked out over the standing-room-only crowd, I said, "I would like to tell you what it is really like over there." You could have heard a pin drop.

By 1968, of course, anti-war protests had become quite vocal. Our soldiers were being accused of taking part in an immoral war. When they returned home, they were called names, they were spit on and they were reviled.

But here is what I saw: I saw hundreds of soldiers—most who hadn't chosen to be there—living out their faith under very harsh conditions. I saw soldiers living faithful lives, becoming stronger in their faith. We shared some deeply spiritual moments during our jungle church services, all of us so very far from home.

Some soldiers I saw only in passing, but others, like this young man from Iowa, I knew in a personal way. I know that he was faithful to the end. God put me at that little Methodist church that day to comfort a grieving family—and to be comforted myself—in a wonderful way.

Chaplain Richard Martin served 24 years as a United Methodist chaplain for the U.S. Army. After retiring, he ministered on the staff of Hyde Park United Methodist Church in Tampa, Florida, where he directed senior adult ministries, and he conducts services as a volunteer at his retirement community. He served in Vietnam and has had many stateside and overseas assignments, including Thailand, Korea and Germany. He and his wife, Patricia, live in Gainesville, Florida. They are the parents of three daughters and have three grandchildren.

26

SEARCHING FOR SCOTT

CHAPLAIN DAVID ALEXANDER

LIEUTENANT, U.S. NAVY (MARINES)

Scott is the consummate United States Marine. He has the short, powerful frame of an English bulldog, the long-time mascot of the Corps. He is as quick with his wry smile as he is with his rifle in a firefight. After two combat tours, Scott has seen plenty of those. He exudes confidence, forged in the sands of Parris Island and the rigors of war, but he doesn't talk about either much. He'd rather live in the present moment and share in a joke.

Scott grew up in the suburbs of New York City, and his family still lives there and attends St. Anthony's Orthodox Church in Bergenfield, N.J. I was assigned to his parish while attending St. Vladimir's Seminary in New York. The first time I met Scott, he was just returning from Iraq, and his parents invited me to his "coming home" party at their house. I got hopelessly lost trying to find their house. I must have called Scott's father ten times for directions!

Ever since then, it feels like I have been continually searching for Scott in one place or another. Soon after he left New Jersey that Sunday afternoon to head back to Camp Lejeune, I received orders from the Navy Chaplain Corps stationing me with the Marines just down the street from Scott. Our command buildings were less than a half mile from each other, but getting together wasn't so easy. We stay pretty busy in the Marine Corps.

Eventually, after a series of phone calls and near misses over my first months at Camp Lejuene, Scott and I finally got together on the base, and then my wife and I had him over to our house for dinner. Scott became a regular at my little Orthodox chapel at nearby Camp Johnson.

Last fall, I realized I hadn't seen Scott in a couple of weeks. I called his cell phone, but got no answer. With a little digging, I found out he was at a training exercise across the country. When he returned, I was traveling west for training of my own. Again, we missed each other. After that, I was deployed to Afghanistan. Through the grapevine, I heard that his battalion was soon to follow.

When Scott's battalion arrived in Camp Leatherneck, a staging point for Marines in Afghanistan, I was there visiting some of my own Marines. I set out in the dead of night to find him, knowing he was just passing through and anxious to see him before he was out of my reach. I walked a couple of kilometers in the dark, stopping to ask directions several times at burn barrels, where Marines huddled for warmth and conversation.

Little by little, I made my way to the transient tents where his company was staying. I woke up sleepy Marines in at least five different tents before one of them pointed to a silhouette on a cot. It was Scott!

Scott seemed completely unsurprised to see me, as blasé as ever at being in Afghanistan, and we agreed to meet in the morning. When we did, I brought him Communion. We headed over to the dining tents for breakfast, talking about family and his battalion and where he was headed. I anointed him with oil in preparation for the battle that he faced in just a few hours.

A few weeks later, I got word that an Orthodox soldier operating in the area had been injured in an attack and had been flown to a surgical hospital near me. It took some time before I learned that he was in an overflow tent located in a small lot behind the hospital. As I was praying with this soldier, in a tent full of Army soldiers, a lone Marine uniform caught my eye. It was Scott! His face and neck were swathed in bandages, but his trademark smile was unmistakable.

Scott had been injured in a Taliban attack and flown by helicopter to the same hospital, and the same tent, as the soldier I was visiting. What were the chances? I anointed him and read the Holy Unction service, but soon I had to leave to attend to some other business. I promised Scott I'd come back later in the evening.

When I returned that evening, though, the tent was completely empty. The medical staff told me that Scott had been transferred elsewhere for the night, but no one was quite sure where. His wounds, I was grateful to hear, were mostly superficial.

It was late, so I returned to my own tent. The next day, I woke up saying to myself, "Today, I have a single mission—to find Scott!"

Finding him was, as always, an adventure, but I was eventually pointed in the right direction by a corpsman and a Marine who knew him. As I approached his cot inside a huge transient berthing tent, he was listening to an iPod®, bopping his head along to the music and seeming in good spirits. Again, I served him Communion and we talked about the attack.

Scott's squad had been on a foot patrol in a pretty dangerous area. An explosion had thrown him in the air and shrapnel had cut into his neck and body. While his squad tended to his wounds and prepared for the MedEvac helicopter to retrieve him, they came under heavy rifle fire and a few of his squad members were also wounded.

I have always been impressed by Scott's toughness, but never as much as that morning. Even as he told his story, he was calm and steady, eager to rejoin his brothers in one of the most unstable regions of Southern Afghanistan. He would rejoin them as a recipient of our nation's oldest military decoration, one instituted by George Washington in 1782 to recognize American warriors wounded in battle—the Purple Heart. All in all, it seemed to me that Scott was going to be just fine. I'm just thankful he is on our side.

I was delighted that Scott's helicopter transport back to his unit was postponed by mechanical difficulties and he was able to celebrate Pascha (Easter) with the Orthodox Christian community at Camp Leatherneck. We had about 45 people in all, including some soldiers from the Republic of Georgia. My heart was full as Scott approached the chalice for Communion.

Searching for people is mostly what I do here. I am the only Orthodox Christian chaplain in the country for any branch of service, and I travel all over to find people—including soldiers from nine different NATO countries. Orthodox families from across America, Canada, and even Australia, ask me to find their sons and daughters in Afghanistan and bring them some peace in the midst of war. It seems I am always searching for someone, searching for something.

Sometimes I find them, and sometimes I don't. Sometimes, I find them and can't get to them. Sometimes, a soldier doesn't particularly want to be found. In such times, I often find myself talking to someone else, someone who really needs somebody to lean on, somebody to show them the face of God in the valley of the shadow of death, someone I never would have met if I had stayed put.

The truth is that, left to my own wisdom, I don't know much of anything about where I am needed. Whatever I have searched for on my own in this life, with a few exceptions, has seemed more important at the time than it turned out to be in reality. The searching just keeps me mobile, I think. If I can hold the object of my search loosely, and orient my heart even the tiniest bit to God along the way, He fills it to overflowing with his grace, and whatever comes of the search, it is enough.

Even now as I write this, dirty and tired and baked by the sun, missing my wife and my little girl so much that my stomach aches when I think of them, it strikes me that I don't remember all of what it was that brought me here; I don't remember much of what I thought I was searching for in becoming a chaplain. I just see God's favor written under my entire life, through the easy times and through the fog of heartbreak and the disillusionment. I see it here in this dark and weary land full of confusion and death just as clearly as I ever have. Looking back, and looking forward, there is only God.

Chaplain David Alexander is an Antiochian Orthodox priest and Navy chaplain assigned to the United States Marine Corps at Camp Lejeune, North Carolina. Father Alexander has been deployed to Helmand Province, Afghanistan, in support of Operation Enduring Freedom and shares his experiences in his bi-weekly podcast "In the Valley of the Shadow of Death," produced by Ancient Faith Radio, from which this story is excerpted and adapted with permission. He and his wife, Heather Maria, live in Cedar Point, North Carolina, with their daughter Eve Marie.

27

TINING FOR HOME

CHAPLAIN BRAD LEWIS

CAPTAIN, U.S. ARMY

I can't imagine there is anyone here in Iraq who doesn't want to go home. There's no question—it's very fulfilling to be a part of something so big and to play a role in the freeing of an entire nation. But war is unrelenting. Whether it's an aircraft zipping overhead, the rapid ping of gunfire, or the thump of an explosion, it doesn't stop. Even in moments of relative silence, war hangs in the air.

All in all, it's pretty much like Dorothy says: "There's no place like home." If only we could click our heels and be back in Kansas or Georgia or California or Maine.

Despite our circumstances, they treat us pretty well here, especially at chow time. Because soldiers are on differing schedules, most chow halls offer not a mere three meals a day but an impressive four meals a day: breakfast, lunch, dinner, and the ever popular and name-free midnight meal. They try hard to make the food taste like home. Each meal offers a variety of foods—veal, green beans, burritos, chicken. Lots and lots of chicken.

But there are some things that just can't be replaced. As I sit down for meals and talk with soldiers—about life, military service, home, families, children, whatever—everyone misses something. For one soldier, it's drinking coffee from his favorite mug. For another, it's the morning newspaper. Still another soldier will miss the smell of his children, or maybe the taste of his mom's lasagna.

Everyone misses something. Everyone looks forward to getting back to that something. Everyone dreams of normalcy. That's where the sacrifices of our servicemen and women can be very clearly seen, in the little things they willingly give up to live and work in this rat hole. Yet they don't complain or whine or blame anyone. They just keep fighting and working and dreaming of going home. These are some truly great people.

Like the next guy, I, too, want to go home and hold my wife and play with my kids. I want to sip coffee from my own mug. I want to work in my own yard. But having been deployed to several locations in a very short period of time, I find I miss one thing more than anything else.

Forks.

I miss forks. For me, plastic is the problem. It's those silly plastic forks with the hollow tines. That's what we use over here.

Everything you eat gets jammed in the tines. The fork feels funny in your mouth. It breaks when you try to spear something.

I miss real silverware. Ahhh! The feel of smooth aluminum or steel or tin or silver, whatever they make silverware out of. I'm no utensil-ologist, but I know a good fork when I see one. For me, knives and spoons are not an issue. Forks are what I miss.

Like I said, I'm no different than the next guy. But, unlike the next guy, I have the perfect spouse. She knows me and she loves me anyway. She listens to my complaints.

Recently, I was home just long enough to drive my kids to school a couple of times and kiss my bride. And just before I took off again for parts unknown, she bought me a fork.

A fork! It's not a fancy fork, and it's not a girly fork. It's a perfect fork. It has a nice big manly black-and-silver handle. It's easy to hold onto, and it has perfectly straight and smooth tines. I love my fork.

In the middle of the madness here, you have to look for something—anything—you can hang your sanity on. So, now, when I go to eat breakfast or lunch or dinner or just have an afternoon snack, I reach into my pocket and pull out my little friend, and we enjoy a meal together. You're right, Dorothy, there's no place like home. Even when it's the size of a fork.

Chaplain Brad Lewis is a U.S. Army chaplain endorsed by the Assemblies of God. In his military career, he has been deployed to Iraq. He and his wife, Tina, have four children; Samuel, Mason, Wyatt and Olivia. "Tining for Home" is excerpted and adapted with permission from Training for Eternity, a blog Chaplain Lewis wrote while deployed.

28

SAILOR ON THE RUN

CHAPLAIN DUDLEY JOHNSON

COMMANDER, U.S. NAVY, RETIRED

I'm going to tell you this story, and I want you to know that I think this is a very funny story—at least I do now. But when it was happening, believe me, it wasn't funny at all!

In 1986, I was stationed on a combat support ship, the USS *Camden*. We were going out to sea, steaming off the coast of San Diego. One day, I was called to the Master at Arms office. These are the folks who provide security services while you're at sea. When I arrived in the MA's office, he was there with a sailor who was threatening to commit suicide.

The MA had restrained the sailor physically, as he wasn't being cooperative, to put it mildly. We called for the doctor to meet us and administer a sedative to the sailor, and then the three of us planned to get the fellow to sick bay.

Now, the Master at Arms office is in the aft of the ship, while sick bay is in the fo'c'sle, which is in the bow. The USS *Camden* is 900 feet long, the length of three football fields. It's a long walk from one end to the other.

We talked about how we were going to get the sailor to sick bay. He was a tall, gangly guy, and he weighed about 190 pounds. The MA and I could hold him down while the doctor administered the shot. But getting him to sick bay was another matter. The doctor couldn't help all that much—he had a birth defect that had withered one of his arms so that it looked like a bird wing. In a bit of typical military humor, we called the doctor "Wings."

Assessing the situation, the doctor decided not to inject the sailor, but instead walk him up to sick bay unsedated, allowing him to keep his dignity as much as possible. So we grabbed hold of him and started on our way.

Well, as soon as we got out of the MA's office, the sailor broke away and bolted up the ladder. He turned right and headed for the rear of the ship, under the flight deck. Behind him, we all started sprinting to catch up with him.

When he got to the back of the ship, without hesitating for a moment, he leaped off the railing. Right below the sailor lay the giant screws that rotate on shafts, controlling the ship's speed. The *Camden*'s screws were 23 feet in diameter, and there were two of them side by side. That's 46 feet of screw space. If he fell into the screws, the sailor would be chopped up like liver.

But just as the sailor jumped, I reached out and grabbed for him and caught him by the shirt. At the same time, the MA reached out and grabbed him by the other side of his shirt. His weight pulled us down over the side, but we held on by our feet, dangling over the edge of the ship.

Unbelievably, at that very moment, a helicopter came in to land on the ship. The captain of the *Camden* had been out and was bringing in some fellow captains.

So, now the helicopter is hovering above us while we're struggling to keep our balance. If we don't hang on, we all go over the edge into the screws. But the downdraft from the helicopter is so strong, the sailor begins to swing like he's on a pivot. I knew I couldn't hold on for very long like that, certainly not as long as it would take to shut down the helicopter.

Hanging off the edge of the ship, I was scared to death. Looking down, I'm thinking, *This is it! We're all going in! I'm going to die.*

Just then, "Wings" reached out with his good arm and pulled the sailor back into the ship, fighting hard against the downdraft. Quick as lightning, he jabbed the sailor with a needle, and in an instant the sedative turned him into a zombie. Believe me, we hustled him back to sick bay as fast as we could and locked him up good.

It was my job to brief the captain after the incident. I knocked on the hatch, but he was in with the other captains, so I went down to the Executive Officer's office to wait for him. A few minutes later, the captain came in.

As I began to tell the captain what had happened, this sudden urge to laugh hit me. It was all I could do to keep from laughing out loud as I briefed him. It was a nervous reaction. I was so relieved to be alive! The captain decided that since we were four days out at sea, the sailor should be handcuffed to his rack until we could put ashore and get him to the naval hospital in San Diego. So that's what we did.

As I think back on my brush with death, it wasn't like in the movies, when someone's life flashes before their eyes. It all happened so fast, there wasn't time to reflect on the transition from life to death. I was working too hard to keep that transition from happening! I was just fighting for my life. Even afterward, I basically had just one thought: "I'm alive! Thank God I'm alive!" And that's a thought I have to this day. I was—I am—so thankful to be alive.

Chaplain Dudley Johnson served in the Marine Corps during the Vietnam War, after which he felt a call to ministry. Following his college career, he attended seminary and pastored several United Methodist churches in Oregon and California. He was appointed to the Navy Chaplain Corps in 1981 and retired from the military in 2004. He has a daughter and two sons, and he and his wife, Janet, have four children.

29

The Rockets' Red Glare

CHAPLAIN JASON HESSELING

MAJOR, U.S. ARMY

And the star-spangled banner in triumph shall wave
O'er the land of the free and the home of the brave!

FRANCIS SCOTT KEY,

"THE STAR-SPANGLED BANNER"

The Fourth of July has always been one of my favorite celebrations. I love the fireworks, the barbeques, heading out on the lake and spending time with the family.

But holidays are difficult times when you're deployed. The year I was deployed to Afghanistan, we did what we could at FOB Sharana to make up for it. We planned a July 4th barbeque outside the chow hall, setting up a grill and erecting a huge cargo parachute to provide shade, anchoring it with picnic tables.

But the day didn't go as we had planned. It started the night before with incoming. We heard a few whistles, a couple of explosions, and we all looked up thinking, "Fireworks!" But quickly we realized these weren't fireworks, so we headed for the bunkers. Thankfully, no one was hurt.

But on the morning of the 4th, there was a major attack at one of our smaller bases bordering Pakistan. We lost two soldiers in the attack and seven were wounded. Those killed in action came to us at Sharana. I spent my day at the hospital praying over them, talking to their buddies and squad members, and coordinating the ramp ceremony for fallen heroes and their angel flight home.

My assistant and I then headed off to the command observation post that suffered the attack. We shored up physical defenses, repairing the bunkers, filling countless sandbags and positioning them on the roof, all while dressed in full body armor in 90+ degree heat. We also shored up spiritual defenses, working with the company commander and friends of the fallen heroes as they prepared the soldiers' memorial service, helping them find the words to pay due honor to their friends. We offered spiritual counseling, shared words of faith, even prayed for our enemies. We prayed for hope and courage in combat.

This is one of the toughest jobs of a chaplain, to give hope and life in the face of death. I don't like going in that room, I don't like praying over a flag-draped coffin, but I do so because I firmly believe what my faith teaches about this moment: that death is not an end but a transition; that, as it says in the Bible, when our earthly house is destroyed we gain an eternal home in heaven, one not made by human hands. As a priest, I point to the presence of hope and grace in the darkness of grief. Hope and grace are present not because of me, but because of the One who prepares that everlasting home for us.

The day after the attack, we had our usual Sunday mass, and then caught lunch at the main DFAC. Outside they still had the grills set up for the July 4th barbeque, so they fired them up again. But right around lunch-time, the wind started blowing and it caught the parachute overhead. The lift capacity of these parachutes is pretty big—three of these things can hold up a Humvee. So, suddenly picnic tables started flying through the air! Thankfully, all we lost were the brats and burgers we abandoned as we ran for safety.

The rest of the day we spent quietly, lounging around, playing volleyball and cards and pigging out at the snack table. It was a typical family reunion, except I wasn't related to anyone and everyone was wearing green. It was a day of some much needed rest, though a somber day, one overshadowed by the deaths of our two soldiers.

A couple of centuries ago, on July 4, 1776, fifty-five men gathered in Philadelphia to share their idealistic and traitorous thoughts about freedom. In time, all of these men would stake their families, their fortunes and their lives on the notion that there must be a better way to govern a nation, that freedom is important enough to fight for, that a life of fear and bondage was not what God had in mind.

Since that fateful Fourth of July, our nation has been calling forth her young men and women to stake their lives and their futures on the principles espoused by the Declaration of Independence. They step up and defend the rights and freedoms of our nation's citizens. Every soldier knows the risks they face each day as he or she pulls on that uniform. Every soldier understands the sacrifices that he or she may be asked to make to bring success to the mission at hand.

For most of us, the sacrifices are a few years of our life, the loss of a few freedoms, the straining of relationships back home, and the hardships of living and fighting in an unpleasant part of the world. But some offer a much higher sacrifice than others. Some lose their jobs or their families while off fighting the war, and some suffer physical and mental wounds. Some lay down their lives on the altar of freedom.

Great or small, every sacrifice of every soldier is reflected in and honored on the Fourth of July. Personally, I agree with a battle buddy of mine, a fellow chaplain who believes we need to put some loudspeakers on the chapel roof and when the mortars start coming in, we should blast the Star-Spangled Banner back at them. Our national anthem is a reminder that this is not the first time American soldiers have been under fire, nor will it be the last. We can handle this, and the flag will still be flying when the rockets are silent. Just ask Francis Scott Key.

Chaplain Jason Hesseling is a Catholic priest ordained in the Diocese of Madison, Wisconsin, serving as an Army chaplain for the Archdiocese for the Military Services. Prior to his commissioning in 2008, Father Hesseling served parishes in Mazomanie and Mill Creek, Wisconsin. During his year-long deployment to Afghanistan, Father Hesseling kept an online journal, Centurion Faith, from which this story is excerpted and adapted. Father Hesseling is the son of an Airborne Ranger who served two tours in Vietnam and has two brothers, one of whom has served in the Wisconsin National Guard. His mother is an active volunteer at Father Hesseling's hometown parish church in Platteville, Wisconsin.

30

A MARINE'S PRAYER

CHAPLAIN DEBORAH LUETHJE MARIYA

LIEUTENANT COMMANDER, U.S. NAVY, RETIRED

If there's one thing I learned as a Navy chaplain, it is this: Never doubt the power of prayer.

A young Marine came into the hospital during my time as chaplain at the National Naval Medical Center in Bethesda, Maryland. He couldn't have been more than 18 or 19 years old. He'd only been in the service six months, a year tops.

This young man was facing a life-threatening cancer. It was a tumor on his spine. It could not be treated conventionally, with chemotherapy or radiation. The only recourse was surgery. And, after the surgery, his life could be changed forever. He could be unable to have sexual relations or he could be paralyzed and never walk again. It was possible he would not survive the procedure. But he definitely would not survive without it.

I got to know this young man in the weeks after he was admitted to the hospital and his doctors began their testing and the process of reaching a diagnosis. When the doctors finally gave him the diagnosis and told him of the surgery and its risks, he was stunned. Every outcome was difficult news for this young man to hear. But he knew he had to go through it, even if there was no good outcome.

Throughout his stay in the hospital, the young Marine and I prayed together in his room. On the night before the surgery, his family and friends gathered there to talk and pray. We prayed like never before. The young Marine opened his heart and his life completely to God. He was not only praying, but also saying his final goodbyes—goodbyes to his girlfriend, and to the friends and family he feared he might never see again.

The morning of the surgery, the hospital gathered its four teams of surgeons. They were facing 24 hours of surgery for this delicate procedure. The team had been assembled from several area hospitals—they were the most experienced surgeons in their fields.

Just before they wheeled the young man away to be prepped, we prayed again, a short prayer, all of us together. Then, his family left the hospital, as it would be hours before they would hear how the surgery was going. I remained at the hospital and went about my work.

Barely an hour later, the lead surgeon called me into the recovery room. They had brought the Marine out of surgery already. I was stunned. *How bad could the news possibly be?* I wondered.

As the Marine started to come around from the anesthetic, the doctor held out his hands, palms up, in a gesture I couldn't really read.

"The tumor's gone," he said, simply.

The Marine replied with gratitude. "Thank you, doctor!" he said.

But the doctor shook his head.

"Hey, we didn't do anything," he said. "The tumor is just gone."

It was unbelievable. When the hospital called the family back in and gave them the news, they were confused. "Do you remember who we are?" they asked. "Are you sure you've got the right patient?"

After all the MRIs, the CT scans and medical tests the Marine had gone through, there was no doubt they had the right patient. And there was no doubt that he had had a life-threatening tumor. Yet it was gone. It was undeniable!

There is power in releasing ourselves to God, in surrendering to his care. God can—He does!—break into our lives. Miracles do happen! I know because I saw one.

Chaplain Deborah Luethje Mariya is a retired Navy chaplain ordained by the Iowa Annual Conference of the United Methodist Church. In addition to her time at the National Naval Medical Center, Rev. Dr. Luethje Mariya also served tours aboard the USS Cape Cod, Amphibious Squadron 5, CCAT US Pacific Fleet, Naval Security Station, Washington, D.C., and Arlington National Cemetery. She is a veteran of Desert Storm and of operations in the Philippines and Haiti. She has also served congregations in Iowa, California, Maryland and Athens, Greece. She lives in Coronado, California, with her husband, Sam J. Tangredi, Ph.D., a retired Navy captain, and their 7-year-old daughter, Mercy.

31

MY SOUL IS SAFE

CHAPLAIN WAYNE GARCIA
MAJOR, U.S. ARMY

Precious in the sight of the Lord is the death of his saints.

PSALM 116:15

To many soldiers, a chaplain is sort of like a rabbit's foot. They like to have us around. When we get into a convoy with them they often will say, "We're good to go! We've got the Chap with us!"

But it doesn't always work that way.

In November 2003, I was deployed to Iraq as brigade chaplain for the 3-2 Stryker Brigade Combat Team, the first Stryker brigade of the Army. Six months into my deployment, I was asked to go to a particular forward operating base to provide a Palm Sunday service. The chaplain there, one of my battalion chaplains, was on emergency leave.

The road to this FOB was typically dangerous. Improvised explosive devices (IEDs) were a distinct possibility. But our convoy arrived there okay and I held the service as planned. That evening, the four vehicles of our convey—two Humvees, a Stryker and a Light Medium Tactical Vehicle (LMTV)—started back to our FOB.

At one point on the route, the road passed under a bridge. It was held up by two supporting columns. Our convoy passed the first column and then at about 5:15 p.m, just as our Humvee passed the second column, a huge blast reverberated all around us. A deep roaring sound rumbled through my chest and the bridge was instantly engulfed in clouds of billowing smoke.

"Oh, God, we've been hit!" our gunner cried. Inside our vehicle, though, we were all okay. Quickly, I got out and looked around. I saw two men walking away from us toward a herd of goats and sheep.

I knew that soldiers must have been injured, so I ran back under the bridge. When I got there, I saw an injured female soldier lying face down on the windshield of the upturned LMTV and a male soldier being pulled out of it. The solider on the windshield was alone, so I went to help her. She'd been hit very badly in the legs. The combat medic arrived seconds later and started an IV on her. I assisted by holding up the IV.

She was crying out in pain and asked for water, so I gave her some from my canteen. I asked her if I could pray with her and she said yes. So, I prayed out loud, I talked to her, and I quoted scriptures to soothe her. Psalm 46:1 is a verse that I always want a wounded soldier to hear: "God is our refuge and strength, an ever-present help in trouble."

By the time I finished, more Strykers had arrived and sealed off the corridor. Eventually, Kiawah choppers arrived for air security and combat engineers scoured the area for more IEDs. They found that two IEDs had been planted under the bridge, one next to each supporting column, and they were daisy-chained together, so that when detonated, both IEDs went off at the same time. I believe the IEDs were planted and detonated by the two men among the herd of goats and sheep, but they were not caught.

In spite of the medic's attempts to save the other soldier who was hit, he was already gone. About 40 minutes later a MedEvac chopper arrived. We helped the female soldier onto a stretcher and loaded her onto the chopper. I prayed again for her and for the other soldiers as the MedEvac bird lifted off.

It was only then that I realized how to close to death I had come myself. Until then, I had given no thought to myself. Now, suddenly, I started to well up with tears. But this was not the time to lose it, so I held my tears back. I looked around, and I saw blood everywhere—American blood. In that instant, I shut off all my emotions except anger. I had only one thought in my head: *I am not going to let the enemy see one drop of American blood on this soil.*

While the others began recovering equipment, I started to shovel dirt over every drop of blood I could see. I picked up every scrap of paper, every piece of equipment I could find with blood on it. Another soldier joined me and began to help cover up every inch of the scene. We worked at it for about three hours.

When we were done, we went back to the FOB where I had con-ducted the Palm Sunday service. We gathered the soldiers into a room for a debriefing, where we talked out the incident and shared our thoughts and feelings. I closed with prayer and, after that, waited for a convoy to take me back to my FOB.

I tell you, I did not want to go back underneath that bridge. But it was the only route back to my FOB. Approaching the bridge, I became more and more anxious. As we drove through the underpass, my insides screamed out. If I had a brake in front of me, I would have slammed it down. It was all I could do to contain my emotions.

Emerging from the other side, I felt my whole body relax. But that night, I didn't sleep well. I woke early in the morning and watched the sun rise and wept for the soldier who had died. I thanked God for being alive another day, so aware that my comrade had not lived to see this day. I prayed for the injured soldier, that she would make it.

A few days later, the brigade surgeon came up to me. "Padre," he said, "I have some bad news for you."

He told me the wounded soldier had died on a MedEvac flight earlier that day. A blood clot hit her heart and she died instantly. The news just tore me up. I wept unashamedly for her.

The soldier's battalion chaplain held a memorial ceremony for her. When I arrived, I was handed a bulletin. Opening it, I looked at her picture and read the information about her life, and a shock ran through me. Her birthday was the same as mine, November 21.

I was hit with another wave of sorrow. I began to well up with tears. Though we shared the same month and day of birth, she was years younger than I was, only 22 years old. And yet now she was gone.

Just before I was deployed to Iraq, I had a dream. In my dream, I was killed in combat and observing the scene from above my body. Oddly, though, I wasn't disturbed by the dream. Rather, I was comforted by it. I sensed the presence of the Lord and was reminded of the Bible verse that says, "Do not be afraid of those who can kill your body, for they cannot kill your soul." I heard God tell me, *Your soul is well, for it is in my care.* From that moment, I lost my fear of death, because I knew my soul was safe in the care of the Lord.

Chaplain Wayne Garcia is a U.S. Army chaplain endorsed by the Church of the Nazarene. He was enlisted in the Air Force for four years in the 1970s and pastored West Hills Church of the Nazarene in Taft, California, before entering the Army Reserve in 2002. In 2004, he became an active duty chaplain. He and his wife, Jody, have seven children.

32

EASTER IN FALLUJAH

CHAPLAIN JOHN MORRIS

MAJOR, MINNESOTA ARMY NATIONAL GUARD

Christ, the Lord, is risen today—Alleluia!

Sons of men and angels say—Alleluia!

Raise your joys and triumphs high—Alleluia!

Sing, ye heavens, and earth, reply—Alleluia!

CHARLES WESLEY,

"CHRIST THE LORD IS RISEN TODAY"

Only once in my life have I conducted an Easter service knowing with certainty that by the end of the day, some of the worshippers in front of me would no longer be living.

After the overthrow of Saddam Hussein, Fallujah was a hot spot in Iraq. In March 2004, four American contractors were ambushed and killed in a particularly grisly way. Within days—on April 4—the Marines launched an offensive against insurgent forces for control of the city and Al-Anbar Province.

Operation Vigilant Resolve was the largest urban combat mission since the Battle of Hue in 1968, one of Vietnam's bloodiest battles.

The fighting was intense: IEDs, rockets, gunfire, explosions, mortar attacks. It was utter chaos.

In the midst of the invasion, I was stationed as chaplain at Camp Blue Diamond, the 1st Marine Division's headquarters, supporting Army psychological operations soldiers. I kept a wary eye on the calendar as Easter Sunday—April 11—approached.

The camp's Catholic priest, Father Devine, and I conferred about Easter services. Of course, by holding a public event you make yourself a target for enemy attacks. This was a distinct possibility here, since the camp was being mortared. Should we imperil lives for the sake of a church service?

Despite the risks, we decided to go ahead and conduct a combined sunrise service, which I planned to follow with a Protestant service in the chapel.

Before the sun rose on Easter Sunday, Father Devine and I turned out on a concrete slab beside a former palace of Hussein's, close by the Euphrates River. Someone had decorated the slab with white flowers indigenous to Iraq—to this day I don't know who. It was an incredible sight in the harshness of the barren desert.

A brass ensemble from the Marine Corp Band came out to play for the service. Soon, in the grey murkiness, we heard the rising strains of the old hymn, "Christ the Lord Is Risen Today."

Marines began to emerge from the foggy darkness, approaching alone and in twos and threes. In all, 56 soldiers gathered, armed and dressed in combat gear for their mission. Father Devine and I spoke urgently about the message of the Resurrection, the certainty that death is not the end for us.

Afterward, we continued our worship inside the chapel. It was a small building, and it was packed to the gills with 125 Marines and a few Army personnel.

The walls of the chapel were lined with large posters of every Marine in Al-Anbar Province who had been wounded or killed—no stained glass here. Marines are proud of their heritage and do not take the death of one of their own lightly.

As I looked around at the posters, a verse of Scripture filled my mind: "*Therefore, since we are surrounded by such a great cloud of witnesses, let us throw off everything that hinders and the sin that so easily entangles, and let us run with perseverance the race marked out for us*" (Heb. 12:1).

I looked into the eyes of these Marines, and I saw their deep hunger for hope. I knew—and they knew—that some of them would not live to see tomorrow's sunrise, would not even see the sun set tonight. They wanted to hear about the Resurrection because their lives depended on it. And so, I began.

"We are facing death," I said. "The enemy is right outside the gate."

"But we can settle the question of death right here today," I told them. "Our life here on earth may be taken from us, but the eternal life that God offers can never be taken away. Because of this certainty, we can serve faithfully and fearlessly."

As I spoke, I could sense spirits lifting, hearts drawn to the power of the Resurrection. I felt their dread, expectancy and joy all melded together. The sight of these young Marines—these sons, these daughters, these fathers, these mothers—lifting up their faces to me pierced my heart. I'd never before, and I've never since, experienced the intensity of worship we shared that day.

Celebrating the Resurrection in Fallujah on Easter Sunday was memorable and beautiful, a sacred privilege. During the days and weeks of fighting that followed, a lot of Marines were killed, a lot of soldiers died. I learned in Iraq that every day is today. We don't have tomorrow. We need the gospel of hope now.

Chaplain John Morris serves with the Minnesota Army National Guard. After ministering as senior pastor at St. Croix Valley United Methodist Church for eight years, he was mobilized in 2004 to serve with Army Special Operations Command. He has been stationed stateside and in Norway, Kuwait, Qatar, Iraq and Cuba. He is co-founder of Beyond the Yellow Ribbon, a military training program for helping Reserve and Guard soldiers and their families learn to reintegrate successfully. Chaplain Morris and his wife, Kathy, have three daughters, Amy, Allison and Anna.

33

THESE SACRED MOMENTS

CHAPLAIN JASON PETERS

MAJOR, U.S. AIR FORCE

Come what come may,

Time and the hour runs through the roughest day.

SHAKESPEARE, *Macbeth:* ACT 1, SCENE 3

On my first night in Kirkuk, I was jolted awake by the sound of .50-caliber machine guns.

In 1999, I was deployed to Kirkuk Regional Air Base in Iraq, serving alongside the 101st Airborne. I had been there just 14 hours and it was pitch black in my pod as I listened to the terrifying sound of close-range gunfire. It was 4:30 in the morning.

Somebody's trying to get onto the base! I thought. But I didn't really know what was happening. I was alone in my trailer, so I didn't have anyone to ask. For the first time, I realized the gravity of the situation I was in. Most forward operating bases are pretty remote, but we were right in the middle of the city. Someone could easily lob a hand grenade over the wall.

I got up and quickly struggled into my full body armor and helmet and waited. All was silent. But, of course, I couldn't get back to sleep.

A few hours later, I was grateful to discover that our perimeter had not been attacked that morning, that the gunfire I heard was the sound of soldiers going out on patrol testing their weapons. No one had warned me that this was normal.

My relief was short-lived, however. A few minutes later a call broke out on the radio indicating a dust off, meaning that casualties were inbound. It was an IED, an improvised explosive device. A vehicle had been blown up by a roadside bomb. Three soldiers had been killed on the spot.

This was my first experience in a combat situation and I knew they needed me at the emergency room. I rushed over to the Expeditionary Medical Squadron just as one of our chaplain assistants was helping transport two patients off the UH-60 evacuation helicopter. If you've ever watched the opening of the television show M*A*S*H, that's what the scene looked like.

I sent up urgent prayers for stamina and courage. I could feel the adrenaline surging through my body. I squared my shoulders and entered the emergency room.

One of the soldiers was dead, and the other was badly hurt. Blood covered the emergency room floor around him. I watched silently as our medical professionals valiantly attempted to save him. They tried for what seemed like an eternity to resuscitate him, but they could not.

The mood was somber as the doctor pronounced the soldier dead. A fellow chaplain stepped forward and offered a prayer for the soldier, his family and the troops he served with. He was calm as he prayed, and he demonstrated a confidence that I certainly didn't feel at that moment.

Medical technicians readied the soldier's body for transfer to the mortuary. I joined a captain and a young lieutenant from the mortuary affairs team and we drove over. There, the senior installation chaplain and I walked into the mortuary together.

The four fallen soldiers were brought in. Each soldier had to be positively identified by a member of his unit. Looking over his fallen friend, one young soldier was overcome by emotion. He stormed out of the room, blinded by tears of rage in his eyes. The other chaplain quietly followed him out.

As the bodies were prepared, I placed my hand over each soldier and prayed over him. I thanked God for the soldier's faithful service and asked that He would grant divine peace and comfort to his family. I knew that soon each family would experience their worst nightmare—that heavy knock on the front door. I knew that the Army Casualty Notification Center in Washington, D.C., had already received a call about the incident and would soon dispatch teams to the soldiers' homes. My heart sank at the realization. I have seen that grief in a family's eyes.

I concluded each of my four prayers with a plea that the soldier would rest in peace. *Amens* echoed through the small room.

At 3:15 the next morning, I watched as a blacked-out C-130 Hercules aircraft taxied and parked in preparation for our hero mission. Over 400 airmen and soldiers faced each other in formation and saluted as four flag-draped body transport cases were carried down the line and loaded onto the plane. As the C-130 lifted into the dark skies, we sent prayers up with the brave soldiers who had paid the ultimate price to secure freedom for a people halfway around the world.

With that, my first duty day had ended.

I cannot tell you even half of the horrors of that day. God, in his providence, knew that I would need his strength to face it.

Touching ground in Iraq less than 24 hours earlier, I had wondered what God had in store for me on this tour of duty. What would the ministry of a chaplain look like in a combat environment? I had no idea.

As the chaos unfolded around me that day, I found myself questioning why I was even there. What was my role? I wasn't a doctor. I couldn't save any lives. What difference would my presence make to anyone? *Do I even belong here?* I thought to myself. I was wracked with doubts.

But as the day ended, I realized that a chaplain serves as a reminder of the Holy in a place that desperately needs that knowledge. We hold a soldier's hand, we cradle his head as he takes his last breath. When a chaplain prays over a soldier, everybody stops, everybody bows their heads. We share a very sacred moment together. A chaplain's presence at this moment is powerful. This is what the chaplaincy is all about.

Chaplain Jason Peters is an Air Force chaplain endorsed by the Bible Churches Chaplaincy. He has served as a hospital chaplain and as a chaplaincy instructor. He was deployed to Saudi Arabia during Operation Southern Watch and Diego Garcia as part of Operation Enduring Freedom. He and his wife, Kimberly, have five children, Brittany, Wesley, Tiffany, Lindsay and Jack.

34

A Young Chaplain's Decision

CHAPLAIN EV SCHRUM

COLONEL, U.S. AIR FORCE, RETIRED

One day, a sharp-looking Senior Master Sergeant approached me in a parking lot while I was heading for my car at Randolph Air Force Base in San Antonio where I was deputy command chaplain.

"You probably don't remember me," he said.

But after he jogged my memory, I did remember him.

Years ago—seventeen years earlier, in fact—we were stationed together at Andersen Air Force Base on Guam. He was a young airman then. One day, he asked for an appointment with me. When the day for the appointment arrived, he walked into my office with a young Guamanian woman of Chamorro descent.

These two young people wanted to be married. They were both Catholic, but they could not find a priest who would perform the ceremony. The issue was the couple's timeframe. To honor the commitment of marriage, the Catholic Church usually requested a six-month lead time before they would agree to marry a couple. This young man was due to be shipped out to another assignment soon and if the couple wasn't married, she couldn't go with him.

The couple asked if I would consider marrying them. At first, I wasn't inclined to perform the ceremony either. As a young chaplain, and as a Protestant chaplain, I didn't want to offend anyone or step on any toes. And I had my own requirements, a time commitment of three months for marital counseling. They wanted to be married within a month.

Though I didn't promise anything, I asked if they would be willing to go through a series of counseling sessions with me, and they agreed. Through our sessions, I came to see that they cared deeply for one another and were serious about marriage. Knowing that, I agreed to do the ceremony.

All of this came back to me now as the two of us talked in the parking lot. He told me that he and his wife had two children and were enjoying a happy marriage. They were active in the Catholic church, which had subsequently blessed their union.

"Thank you," he concluded, "for taking the time all those years ago to counsel us and get us off to a good start."

Three years after this encounter, upon completing an assignment at Air Force headquarters in Washington, D.C., I returned to the same base in San Antonio. While there, I learned that this man had been promoted to chief master sergeant, the highest enlisted rank in the Air Force, and was preparing for his own retirement.

He sought me out one day to ask a special favor. At his retirement ceremony, he said, the Catholic priest at the base chapel where he and his family were active would give the invocation. But he wanted me to participate, too. He wanted to surprise his wife by renewing their wedding vows as part of the ceremony. I said that I would be glad to conduct that part of the ceremony.

It was wonderful to surprise his wife in this way! Joyfully, we repeated the vows I had read so many years before with them. It was a very emotional time for all of us. I had the opportunity to meet his beautiful children, one of whom had recently joined the Air Force. I silently thanked God for giving me patience and insight enough as a young chaplain to help this couple get started on their journey through life together.

Chaplain Ev Schrum was ordained a United Methodist minister in 1973 and served as an Air Force chaplain from 1976 to 2004. Before his military career, he was pastor at a church in Houston, Texas. After retiring from the Air Force, he briefly worked as a hospital chaplain and for four years served as associate pastor of First Methodist Church in Georgetown, Texas. He and his wife, Nelia, have a married son and two granddaughters, Evelyn and Brittney.

35

DIEU VOUS AIME

CHAPLAIN HAROLD CARLSON
COLONEL, U.S. ARMY, RETIRED

In my ministry, I've seen a lot of sorrow and dealt with a considerable amount of death.

I once conducted the funeral of a 10-month-old girl, the daughter of a servicewoman, who suffocated between a bed and a radiator. She lay in her coffin in a beautiful white christening gown. She had what looked like a tear on her cheek. I so much wanted God to give life back to this precious girl!

I was called on one time to lead a memorial service for a soldier who was decapitated by the blade of a bulldozer. During my time at Walter Reed Army Medical Center in Washington, D.C., sometimes, not often, but sometimes we'd have three deaths in a night.

But of all the tragedies I've witnessed, one in particular stands out in my mind. I was stationed as a garrison chaplain at Fort Wainwright, near Fairbanks, Alaska. It was January 29, 1989. We were in the midst of a cold siege—for 17 days, the temperature had reached no higher than 50 degrees below zero.

A two-week field exercise called "Brim Frost" had been going on in the Yukon Training Area, which is an area about the size of New

Jersey. It was a joint U.S.–Canadian winter training exercise involving about 26,000 troops.

Many people felt that because of the weather conditions, the exercise should have been called off. You couldn't see a yard in front of your face. At temperatures that low, something called "ice fog" forms, reducing visibility to almost nil.

Additional paratroopers were flying in that night to support the exercise. Three C-130 Hercules transport aircraft carrying troops and equipment were in the air. The first one landed safely, and the control tower began to guide the second plane in. But something went wrong and at 6:47 p.m. the tower lost contact with the pilot. The plane came in too low and its landing gear caught on a snow bank. The plane slammed into the frozen turf several hundred feet short of the runway, ripping it into three pieces.

My wife was taking a walk at our home about three miles away—she's a Minnesota girl and doesn't mind the cold—when she heard what she later said sounded like tinkling bells. It was the plane crashing, with all its accompanying sounds.

I was called to attend the accident, so I immediately got into my car. Driving was a challenge, though, and when I finally got there, the dead and the wounded were being brought in. I came into the emergency room of the hospital just as one wounded soldier was being carried in.

I felt the cold of the arctic air on his body as they wheeled him in. His fingers were frozen and his ear had been torn off and he was bleeding badly. Sadly, those carrying his gurney dropped it at one point, and the soldier cried out in anguish.

As the medical staff worked feverishly to save this soldier's life, I stepped up to him and placed my hand on his forearm. He was French Canadian and spoke no English. I spoke almost no French. But what little I did know, I spoke to him gently.

"Dieu vous aime," I said, over and over. God loves you.

The one saving grace that kept this tragedy from being worse than it was is the fact that at temperatures of 40 degrees below or colder, jet fuel doesn't ignite. Even so, of the 18 Canadians aboard the plane, nine went on to the next life that night and in the weeks that followed. My soldier was treated and taken to Anchorage. He died from his injuries two days later.

You really can't rank misery. It is painful to accept any demise. As I put my hand on the arm or the forehead of a deceased person and pray, I thank God for the gift of this person's life and for the people he or she has loved. I have always felt my ministry was to the living, to help those who must go on after these deaths. In this, I have strived to be faithful to God and to do my duty for my country.

Chaplain Harold Carlson is a retired U.S. Army chaplain endorsed by the Evangelical Free Church of America. He was associate pastor for an Evangelical Covenant Church before entering the military chaplaincy. He served as a chaplain assistant for three years and as a chaplain for 25 years. He was the first chaplain assigned to the Corps of Engineers. He and his wife, Judy, have six children and 13 grandchildren. He is co-author with his brother, the Rev. Charles Carlson, of a devotional book titled Dawg Gone . . . Movin' On *(Xulon Press, 2008).*

36

OUT OF THE ASHES

CHAPLAIN BARBARA SHERER

COLONEL, U.S. ARMY

The central dining facility in Camp Udairi, Kuwait, is gone. A fire that began in one of the DFAC (dining facility) tents quickly spread to engulf all five tents and completely destroyed them in less than 30 minutes. No surprise there . . . the wind was blowing quite hard and the tents were close together.

After the smoke cleared, and all units checked the status of their soldiers, it was apparent that everyone had made it out alive. Amazing. It was Sunday morning and a service had just concluded, but most of the worshippers had left. A service was scheduled next, and one of the tents would have been packed. During breakfast, all the tents were packed, but not at the time of the fire. Some sharp NCOs pushed military and civilian cooks outside, and propane tanks were removed to safety. Firefighters arrived quickly and kept the flames from spreading to the rest of the camp.

What could have been a major catastrophe merely resulted in the loss of some equipment and soldiers eating MREs (meals ready to eat) for a few days. I call this a miracle. God takes care of his children, even when they are deployed far, far away from home. *Especially* when they are deployed far from home.

But let me tell you the rest of the story. The fire occurred on the Sunday before Ash Wednesday. This is the day many Christians observe the beginning of the season of Lent. It is a time of penitence, as we prepare for Holy Week and Easter. We mark our foreheads with ash as a sign of this penitence. I had planned to offer ashes for Protestant soldiers who wished to observe this ritual. I didn't have any ashes, though. Traditionally, you burn palms from the previous year's Palm Sunday celebration to make ash for Ash Wednesday. I didn't have any. So it seemed to me that the most significant ash to use for this occasion would be ash from the DFAC.

The site was under guard, so I asked an MP to escort me to the firefighters who were working there. Things had calmed down, and they were just watching to make sure there were no flare-ups.

I explained to the officer in charge what I wanted. He agreed it was a very appropriate request. I handed a cup to one of the firefighters, who walked to the rubble, scooped up some ash, and returned to me.

"Is this enough?" he asked.

"Perfect," I replied. I placed the cup in a zip-top bag and headed to my tent.

Two days later I decided to open the bag and see if I needed to crunch up the ashes into smaller pieces. I was digging around in the cup with a plastic knife when I noticed the edge of something metallic. I reached in—and pulled out a cross. A flat, metal cross. It had some dark smudges on it from the fire, but it was otherwise undamaged. I could still read the etching on it: "Jesus is Lord."

I can't even fathom the odds of picking the exact site of that cross out of the acreage destroyed by the fire. It doesn't matter. The message to me is clear: God walks with us through the terrible firestorms of our lives, and we are lifted unharmed out of the ashes. We may be marked in some way, like the cross of ash placed on our foreheads during Ash Wednesday. However, that mark is a symbol of God's love and protection.

I wear that cross now on my dogtags. No matter where the Army may send me, or what God may ask of me, I will cherish this special reminder that God will never leave us alone to face the tragedies in our lives. With God's help, we will always rise out of the ashes.

Chaplain Barbara Sherer is an ordained Presbyterian minister. She served in the U.S. Army Reserve for eight and a half years before being called up for active duty in 1992. In addition to her three deployments to Iraq, she has served overseas in Mogadishu, Somalia, Korea and Germany. This article was published as "Out of the Ashes" in Guideposts magazine (June 2003) and is reprinted by permission of the author.

37

A PERSON OF LIFE

CHAPLAIN WILLIAM "DAVE" LOGAN

CAPTAIN, U.S. AIR FORCE

And the song, from beginning to end,

I found in the heart of a friend.

HENRY WADSWORTH LONGFELLOW,

"THE ARROW AND THE SONG"

If you ask me what day it is here at Balad Air Base in Iraq, I have to stop and think about it. It's a little like the movie *Groundhog Day* here—each day exactly like the last day. Once in a while, though, something crashes through the tedium and makes you realize why you're here.

I'm the night shift chaplain here at the Air Force Theater Hospital. We take care of everyone here—coalition forces, Iraqi civilians, detainees. Soon after I arrived, I came across an Iraqi man who had lost both legs in a suicide bombing attack. Understandably, he was despondent and very withdrawn. Day after day, I made my rounds, but he didn't seem interested in talking to me. We would share a nod of recognition, but I would just move along.

One day as I passed by, though, he just looked like he was ready to talk. Something in me said, *"Stop and talk to this man."* So I pulled up a chair. He spoke very good English. It turns out he was a doctor, Dr. Muhammed. As you might expect, he was in a lot of pain, physically and emotionally. Pointing to where his legs once were, he said, "This is my situation." He told me he felt his life was pretty much over.

As Dr. Muhammed spoke, I thought of the time the apostles Peter and John came across a man at the temple gate who couldn't walk. Peter says to the man, "I don't have any money, but I will give you what I do have." What he had was the power of Jesus Christ of Nazareth.

I asked Dr. Muhammed if I could pray with him. He said yes, and so I did. "God of all people, Sovereign of the Universe, I give thanks for Dr. Muhammed," I began. "I thank you for his life and for his family.

"God, you know that Dr. Muhammed is hurting. You know of the losses he has suffered and the uncertainty of his future. I pray that you will give him strength and comfort and hope. I pray for his healing, and for the healing of his nation. I pray that his country will find peace, that his people can move forward with their hopes and dreams. We thank you, God, for what you will do."

After I had finished, I was astonished to find Dr. Muhammed weeping. As the tears ran down his face, he opened his arms to embrace me.

"No one has ever done that for me before," he said, through his tears.

Several weeks later I was making my rounds through the emergency department. I spotted an Iraqi man laughing and smiling as he talked with several staff members. I didn't think anything of it, until I caught a glimpse of him as I walked by. It was my old friend Dr. Muhammed! He had come back for physical therapy. With a huge smile on his face, he reached out his arms for a hug. Then, he said something I'll never forget.

"I was a person of death," he said. "But you changed me into a person of life!"

I don't know where Dr. Muhammed is today, but I know that it is well with his soul. Yes, it may be like *Groundhog Day* here, but every day God does amazing things!

Chaplain William "Dave" Logan is an Air Force chaplain endorsed by the United Methodist Church. His military career has spanned 11 years. In addition to his time in Iraq, he has been deployed to the Balkans. He is raising two young children with his wife, Beth, has an adult daughter, and has suffered the loss of his son.

38

A JUNGLE RETREAT

CHAPLAIN RICHARD ROJAS

CAPTAIN, U.S. AIR FORCE

What I wanted was a spiritual retreat at a sunny tropical beach where we'd relax, maybe scuba dive, and each day delve deeply into the word of God.

What I got was this: A muddy midnight march through a bitterly cold Honduran jungle, soaked to the bone by a pouring rain and tortured by a cloud of mosquitoes.

In 2005, I was deployed on a humanitarian mission to Honduras with the Joint Task Force-Bravo at Soto Cano Air Base. I was command chaplain, the only one assigned to the base. I got it into my head that I wanted to pull off a retreat to the Bay Islands off the coast.

Much to my surprise, I found out that Army regulations allow chaplains to use military aircraft for this purpose. So, I put word out about the retreat and requisitioned a CH-47 helicopter. That's a huge copter, our military's biggest one.

About 25 people signed up, and on the appointed day we started out for the island of Roatan in high spirits. The Bay Islands are known for their beautiful weather and pristine sandy beaches. We were sure looking forward to a little R&R.

Well, it was November and wouldn't you know it, a huge storm came through. The weather was miserable—cold, wet, rainy. We tried to make the best of it. Some of us went scuba diving anyway, but the visibility was terrible. We couldn't see anything of the island's famed coral reefs. No tropical island paradise for us! We had devotions, but they were halfhearted at best.

After two days, we straggled back to the helicopter and took off for the mainland. It would be a relief to get back to the base, where we had warm clothes and dry land waiting.

But once we were in the air, the cloud ceiling dropped down quickly on us. In this situation, you have two choices: You can fly above the ceiling or ride below it. To fly above, you have to get clearance from a tower, so you won't collide with other aircraft. Our pilot tried repeatedly, but he couldn't raise a response from local towers.

Our only choice then was to fly below, but still the ceiling kept dropping. Soon, the pilot had only one option left.

"Chaplain, we're going to have to set the craft down," he said. "It's too dangerous to be circling around here in the mountains."

Over the mainland, the pilot chose a large, open space in what looked to be a jungle and landed. He tried again to make our plight known over the radio, but again, he had bad news for me.

"We can't get anything on the radio, Chaplain," the pilot advised me. "We might have to sit here all night until the storm lifts."

Just as we were considering this possibility, some local Hondurans appeared out of the surrounding jungle. "Did you break down?" they asked us. Now, my name is Rojas, but I'm not fluent in Spanish. Fortunately, two of the guys with me were, and they were able to relay our dilemma.

One of the Hondurans, a policeman carrying an AK-47, said he could lead us through the jungle to a police station in a nearby town, where we could use a phone to summon a bus that would take us to a hotel. That sounded good to me, but our group was divided, some wanting to stay with the helicopter, some wanting to make the trek. "It's your gig," was all the highest-ranking officer said to me.

I started off with a few of those who liked the idea of a hotel bed and a hot meal. The ones who stayed behind faced a tough night. It was cold in the mountains, but we weren't dressed for it and the helicopter is meant for cargo, so there wasn't anywhere to sleep but benches and the floor. And the mosquitoes were merciless.

We followed the locals out into the jungle. It was pouring rain and the path was muddy. With every step, our feet sank into the mud. No one had on the right foot gear; most wore sandals of some sort. I took off my flip flops and went barefoot.

Pretty soon, we came to a canal, where we had to cross over on a log. The log was slick with rain, but everyone made it over. Everyone except me, that is. I slipped off and fell chest-deep into the muddy water. In my pockets, I carried two cell phones, so we could be in contact with the aircraft. Both were immersed and ruined.

What next? I thought, despair starting to creep into my mind. We were all absolutely miserable—eaten alive by mosquitoes and shivering with the cold. It was so dark we couldn't even see where we were going.

It just can't get any worse than this, I thought as I dragged myself out of the canal. I guess I shouldn't have said that.

Finally, we made it to the police station, which was just a run-down, one-room building. We opened the door and walked in. Inside, there was a bench and a guy sitting at a desk. Nothing else. No phone. *What did we come here for?* I thought with some exasperation.

The policeman said he could take us to a local store to buy a phone card. Down the street we walked until we came to a house. The policeman knocked. Now, by this time it was about 9:30 at night. The store owner came to the door and agreed to open the store. Of course, there were no phone cards in the store. But the man did have a phone.

"Could we give you money to use your phone?" I asked him. He agreed and gave us the number of a local bus operator.

Well, they sure had our number. The bus operator wanted $600 to provide a bus that would take all of us to a hotel. I had no idea whether anyone wanted to shell out that much, but I said yes.

Now, it is the job of senior ranking non-commissioned officers in a situation to advise other officers, even higher ranking ones, on a course of action. The master sergeant in the group had some advice for me now.

"Chaplain, I don't think it's a good idea for us to go back into the jungle to get the others," he said. "I think we should leave them there, get some sleep ourselves, and go back in the morning."

Well, I thought, *I'm not about to leave any of our group behind.* The others were unprotected, sitting out there in the open in that helicopter. It seemed a dangerous situation to me.

"Is there another way back to the helicopter?" I asked the locals. It turns out there was. Someone with a car drove us about a mile to a farm and let us out. Our guides led us through stables, across a farm field and over a gate. Though it was too dark to see, I could tell we were on a cow path—you can imagine how I figured that out.

This time, we trekked through mud and muck a foot and a half deep. We folded our pant legs up, but it wasn't any use. Every few feet, we'd slip and fall down into the mud and have to push ourselves back up. We were covered in mud, head to toe. But eventually, we made it back to the helicopter.

When they saw us, everyone in the helicopter burst out laughing. Frankly, it looked like we'd been to Gehenna and back. Someone snapped a photo while I stood there dripping, a leech attached to one leg.

"Listen, I'm not saying it's easy to get out of here," I said to the group, "but on the other end of this path is a bus waiting to take us to a hotel. I'm going back out to the bus. Who wants to go with me?"

Well, about half of the group chose to go. Of those who stayed, one was a major who was a nurse, and another was a tough Vietnam vet who was used to harsh conditions. About ten people and the three-member crew stayed.

After another long slog on the cow path back through the jungle, we made it out to the waiting bus. The drive was an hour and a half long, but finally we pulled up in front of a motel, with soft beds, clean sheets and hot showers. It was about 1:30 in the morning. There wasn't any food to be had at that hour, so we just fell into bed exhausted but grateful.

The next morning, we were enjoying a hot breakfast when we heard our helicopter approaching. We'd called them the night before to arrange our pick-up. We rushed around getting our gear together and headed outside. The pilot put down on a paved asphalt lot. Cheered from the good food and sleep, I poked my head in the door.

"How'd you all make out last night?" I asked. I was met with groans.

"That was the worst night of my life!" came the answer from one of the guys.

Given the bitter cold and the relentless mosquitoes, sleep was almost impossible. The situation was getting to people and tensions ran high in the helicopter. A fight broke out between a frustrated captain and a major, accompanied by a lot of swearing. One even pushed the other to the ground.

But not everyone shared the same perspective.

"It was a fine night," the Vietnam vet answered. "It was great."

Well, we all got in and took off. We landed at a local airport to refuel, but eventually we made it back to the base, safe and sound.

The next day at our command meeting, amid much smirking and laughter, the deputy commander asked me how the retreat went. Now, those of us in the Reformed tradition believe strongly in the sovereignty of God, so I answered him honestly when I said, "God saved us from the jungle!"

People sometimes think I'm crazy, but I look at life as an adventure. I'm all about fun! I'm a Brooklyn boy. At the age of 18, I was on my way to becoming a professional skateboarder when God called me to himself. He convicted me of my sin, but in my sorrow I found him to be merciful.

That's how I view our "jungle retreat." It was an adventure! And God was merciful to us. I'm not sure that's how the others felt—in the military you generally grouse down, not up to your superiors—but I guess it's no surprise that I haven't been asked to lead another retreat!

Chaplain Richard Rojas is an Air Force chaplain endorsed by the Orthodox Presbyterian Church. In addition to his stateside service, he has been deployed to Honduras and Afghanistan. He and his wife, Deborah, are the parents of four children, Elly, Rich Jr., Kirsten and Trinity.

Major Chuck Weber, flight surgeon on the retreat, was one of those who opted to trek through the jungle with Chaplain Rojas. "I'm former infantry. Rain doesn't bother me," he said. "But I wasn't about to stay with the helicopter. I'd never have gotten any sleep—everybody snores!"

39

START OFF WITH A PRAYER

CHAPLAIN JACK STANLEY
MAJOR, U.S. AIR FORCE

Lord, through this hour

Be Thou Our Guide,

So by Thy power

No foot shall slide.

WESTMINSTER CHIMES

Even though chaplains are deployed to combat zones, Air Force chaplains are rarely deployed outside of Air Force command, but a few rotations do regularly include chaplains. I had one deployment to the Army, and I was sent forward to provide ministry in Afghanistan's Taliban-heavy Kunar province.

Before deploying, I had made a pact with myself. *I'm never going to travel in a convoy unless I have to, because that's where you get blown up!* That was my mantra.

Yes, I was afraid. Chaplains move around between forward operating bases and observation posts to make sure everyone is provided with pastoral care. I always tried to get around by helicopter. I sure didn't want to go by ground unless I absolutely had to. In fact, those were my orders.

During one mission, though, while in the mountainous border region in eastern Afghanistan supporting the Army's 101st Airborne, the Security Forces commander of our provincial reconstruction team asked whether I wanted to join him on a trip to a FOB outside the Korengal Valley. The team was assembling a work crew to repair roads that had been washed away by heavy rains.

This observation post had been attacked several times in the past week. Just a few days earlier, a soldier had been hit in the chest with a bullet that ricocheted down from the mountains. I knew this post could use a visit from a chaplain.

We met the next morning before first light for a mission briefing, and then we were off. The post was about an hour's drive across very bumpy roads that took us through mountain communities. I looked out through the barred windows and was surprised to see so many people along the roads staring at us as we passed. I had never seen this many people in the other places I'd been deployed—Kandahar, Bagram, Bahrain, Kabul, Qatar, Iraq. Endless lines of women walked along in their thick woolen burkas, kids in tow, stopping to watch us. It was as if we were in a parade.

When we got to the post, our commander introduced me to the FOB commander, another captain like myself. I told him I'd be around if anyone wanted to talk. I went over to the tactical operations center, where I got a tour of all the cameras and equipment that gave them a 360-degree view of the surrounding hilltops.

It wasn't long before we heard a low, but definite "Whump!" I looked around. Then I heard another.

Sure enough, we were getting rocketed from the hilltops. With one of the cameras, I zoomed in on where the fire was coming from. Suddenly, a 155-mm. howitzer shell blew up right where I was looking! Even now, it seems odd to me that I had a certain detachment from the scene. Maybe it was the camera.

I spent the rest of the morning talking with a first sergeant who told me stories about life at their remote post. We went to the dining facility for breakfast. It was really just a tent with some mosquito lining and warming trays. There wasn't anywhere to sit, so you'd just grab your meal and go back to your bunk or wherever you were working.

Eventually, we got word that our crew was en route back from the road work. When they arrived, they were discouraged, as only three locals had shown up with a couple of shovels and pick axes. Not the turnout they were hoping for. You have to maintain the roads here, pave them when you can, so that improvised explosive devices can't be hidden in the gravel or dirt. They hadn't made much headway on this dangerous road.

It was time to head back, though, so we piled into our vehicles and went on our way. As we came back down out of the hills and the river road opened out into a clearing, our first vehicle got hit by small arms fire. It was coming from up in the hills ahead of us.

I was in a convoy and we were getting hit! It was exactly what I had always feared. We were sitting ducks out there in the open. The order came down to stop and engage, so soon every gunner in every turret began returning fire. All I could do was pray.

Pretty soon, another patrol came in behind us, Charlie Company from 1st Infantry Division. They are known for their ability to win a fight, and they quickly took the lead, calling in additional support.

After about an hour of shooting, I saw something I never in my life would have believed if I hadn't experienced it. Kids from all over the place started showing up and darting around, grabbing the .50-calibre casings that had landed on the ground. Some of the kids were even running in front of the vehicles while we were shooting, plugging an ear with one hand while they leaned down to pick up the casings with the other. When the big guns started up, they'd run behind our vehicles for protection, waiting for another lull so they could run out and resume picking up the casings.

The word was that these kids would get 25 cents per shell. They probably get repacked or melted down to make mortar rockets to be used against us. They were willing to risk their lives for this.

Finally, an air strike was called in, and we continued our journey home. About four and a half tense hours later, we made it back to our forward operating base. We had a time of debriefing and at the end of it, the lieutenant asked me, "Chap, do you have anything to add?"

In a lighthearted way, I thanked the guys for the adventure of a lifetime. But, in all seriousness, I told everyone how proud I was of them and how honored I was to have made the journey with them. Now I knew what it was to be under attack and I could say, "I understand how you feel." When my life was really on the line, I saw how important it was to take care of the soldiers living on the fringes, to let them know just by being there with them that God loves them.

But something else totally unexpected occurred. This one single event chased the fear from my heart. I am no longer afraid to do my job. Losing your life is a greater threat to your mind than it is in reality. In all honesty, I can't wait for the next opportunity to serve.

Still . . . next time, I'll be sure to start off the mission brief with a prayer!

Chaplain Jack Stanley is an Air Force chaplain endorsed by the United Methodist Church. Prior to his military service, he was in full-time ministry for 12 years as a youth, music and senior pastor in Alabama and Pennsylvania. He has been deployed numerous times to Southwest Asia and Qatar. He and his wife, Stacy, have two children, Scott and Mary Lou.

40

THE GIFT OF LIFE

CHAPLAIN DENNIS ALESON

LIEUTENANT COLONEL, U.S. AIR FORCE, RETIRED

It was Tuesday night, June 25, 1996. Another hot, humid day had come to an end in Khobar Towers, the high-rise housing area at Dhahran, Saudi Arabia, that was home to more than 2,500 coalition forces of Operation Southern Watch following the Gulf War.

I was just one day away from welcoming the chaplain who would replace me as senior chaplain for the 4404th Wing (Provisional), whose mission was to enforce the no-fly zone over southern Iraq. I was excited about heading home to my wife and children.

It had been a long day and I'd just hit a fatigue wall. It was about 10 o'clock at night and I had been awake for 17 hours. I was more than ready to head for bed. I'd been watching the news on television in the chaplains' suite, so I crossed the room to turn off the TV and then headed for my bedroom.

In the instant that I passed under the doorframe into my bathroom, a deafening boom shook the building. The sound of breaking glass followed, as a blast-wave shattered windows and sent shards flying everywhere. The next second, I was plunged into darkness and enveloped in a momentary, deathly silence.

Because of the sudden darkness, my first thought was that a transformer had blown somewhere. But as I backed out of the bathroom into my bedroom, I saw that the large bedroom window I had been facing seconds before was no longer there. All the heavy wooden bedroom furniture had been moved around. This was something more than a power outage.

We did not know it then, but terrorists had exploded a large truck bomb in a Saudi park next to our perimeter fence very close to an apartment building in the complex. Security forces had seen the truck pull up, and then a car pulled up behind it. The occupants of the truck got out and ran to the car, which sped away. An evacuation of the apartment building was already underway. But the blast came in just minutes, with a force of up to 30,000 pounds of TNT.

In the eerie silence that followed the blast, I began to hear indecipherable shouting and yelling. We still didn't know what had happened. Over the public loudspeaker, we were directed to the Desert Rose, the dining facility in the center of the complex, away from the perimeters and probably the safest place to be.

Though my building was close to the decimated building, I was uninjured, as was another chaplain in our suite. We headed out of our building in the darkness, using only the light from my pocket flashlight. We stepped over broken glass, doors that had been blown open and were hanging on their hinges, furniture that had been tossed about. I saw that even a large fuse box had been torn from its mooring in a concrete wall.

Along the way, the Catholic chaplain and I—the only two chaplains in the complex that night—met up with a member of our chapel support staff. When we arrived at the Desert Rose, we saw people who were cut and bleeding. We began to sense the magnitude of what had happened. Quickly, we headed for the medical clinics in the complex, where the wounded were being taken.

What a horrific scene! Hundreds of litters lined the ground outside the clinics, and medical personnel were conducting triage, treating the most serious injuries first. Many of the less seriously wounded airmen were tending to those who were badly injured until they could be seen by medical personnel. Sadly, I was called upon twice to pray over persons who had died, perhaps even before they had been carried to the clinics.

After several hours at the triage center, we headed for the bomb crater site. The blast had left a crater 85 feet wide and 35 feet deep. The entire outside wall of the apartment building was blown away—it looked like the federal building in Oklahoma City that had been bombed just the year before. Many of the victims had already been brought out from the rubble and were being carefully and reverently secured in body bags. I walked among the body bags, praying over each fallen hero. In all, 19 American airmen were killed in the explosion, and many hundreds more were injured.

Finally, it came time to prepare the fallen heroes for their long, sad journey back to America. Several surviving members of the most severely impacted units were brought in to help identify the victims. I stood off to the side as a Lieutenant Colonel, the commander of an air rescue unit, leaning heavily on crutches, opened body bags, looking for five members of his unit.

One of the victims of this unit was the commander's own suite-mate, a captain who had died just ten feet away from him. In the course of evacuating, the commander had gone back into the bedroom of their apartment to get a pair of shoes. The bedroom wall had protected him from the full force of the blast. He was injured and knocked out briefly, but he made his way back to his suitemate in the hallway as he took his last breaths.

Like the commander, my movements in the moments before the blast may also have spared me. I believe the doorframe I was crossing through to get to my bathroom provided extra protection; otherwise, I might have been killed by the implosion of the bedroom window. And, as the other chaplain and I exited the apartment, I saw that the floor-to-ceiling window in the main room had completely shattered. Shards of glass were imbedded in the wall behind where I had been sitting and watching television.

It also stops me in my tracks when I realize that many nights at this very same time, after the heat of the sun had cooled, I was out jogging on the perimeter road just a few yards away from the building destroyed by the blast. In so many ways, I can say that my escape from harm was a narrow one.

Even now, 14 years later, I become emotional thinking about my family at home, hearing almost instantaneously about the blast on television and knowing that airmen were killed, but not knowing whether I was safe. As soon as I could, I put a call through to my house. My son, who was home from college, answered. When he heard my voice, he dropped the phone, and I heard him shout to my wife, "Mom! It's Dad! He's okay!"

Like so many who were essentially uninjured that day, I had feelings of guilt that I escaped unscathed while others a few hundred yards away were killed or gravely wounded. *Why them and not me?* It is a question that to this day I cannot answer. Some people believe that God keeps chaplains free from injury, because of the need for the pastoral care we provide. But for me to say that God showed me special favor over someone else strikes me as a self-righteous presumption.

Rather than try to answer this impossible question, I am simply filled with thanksgiving that I survived. I have been and very much continue to be a recipient of God's blessings and grace. I am thankful that I was able to provide a critical ministry when it was desperately needed. Catastrophic events remind me anew of how fragile life is and what an unmerited gift it is, compelling in me an ever greater, more responsible stewardship and greater service in whatever gift of mortal life remains for me.

Chaplain Dennis Aleson retired in 2003 as an Air Force chaplain after 26 years of service. Chaplain Aleson led the chaplain team response and crisis ministries following the Khobar Towers bombing. A retired United Methodist clergy, he pastored a church in North Dakota prior to his military service, and since his retirement has served as a supply and interim pastor for several churches. He and his wife, Carol, have two adult children, Ryan and Heather, and one grandchild, Calvin.

41

A WHOLE NEW LIFE

CHAPLAIN RICHARD "MIKE" WARNER

LIEUTENANT COLONEL, U.S. AIR FORCE

On a recent deployment, I found myself walking down a busy street in Kampala, the capital city of Uganda. I had just finished up a tour of Christmas ministry—seven locations in five different countries—and was heading back to Camp Lemonnier in Djibouti.

In Uganda, you see a lot of beggars on the street. Unlike in the United States, there are no social services, no welfare systems, no safety nets for the disabled and homeless. Each day, they do what they have to do in order to survive.

I was just outside my hotel when I spotted a man begging. He was among the worst of the worst cases I had seen. This desperate man had no legs. He extended his hands toward me, and I gave him some Ugandan shillings.

But it was pretty clear that God wanted me to do more. I distinctly heard God's voice. He said: *No, I don't want you to just give this man money. I want you to change his circumstances. I want to bring a whole new life to this man.*

I came back with someone who could translate for me, the driver of our vehicle. As U.S. military visiting Uganda, we had hired a driver and a vehicle. It's a precautionary measure. If there ever were an accident and an American military personnel had been driving, we could literally incite a riot. Our driver understood and spoke English fluently, so I told him what God wanted me to do. He was a man of deep faith and he asked if he could help.

When we returned to the sidewalk, we learned that the man's name was Sekerena. He was about 20 years old and a homeless Rwandan refugee. He told us that his village had been attacked by rebels and his entire family had been murdered—his parents, brothers and sisters, wife and children. He saw them all killed and then rebels cut off his legs and left him for dead.

Yet somehow he survived. He had moved to Kampala about a year earlier and was living and begging on the streets.

I knew I had to move quickly. My layover in Uganda was only until the evening, when my flight was scheduled to take off. I talked with a couple of folks who were part of our military team. Pretty quickly, it became clear that my vision for Sekerena meant first finding a wheelchair.

In Uganda, wheelchairs are hard to come by. They're expensive— about $150, which is many months' wages for the average working Ugandan—and they're not easily available. Our military team fanned out and with the help of another Ugandan, we found just two wheelchairs in the whole of Kampala. We bought one at a local bicycle shop.

When I asked Sekerena whether he wanted a wheelchair, he was ecstatic. He smiled wide and said how much the wheelchair would help him. Within an hour, we delivered the wheelchair to him in our Land Cruiser. As he accepted the chair, tears ran down his cheeks, yet his smile just got larger and larger. He reached out his arms to embrace me and thanked us in broken English.

The delivery of the wheelchair drew quite a crowd of onlookers. There must have been 25 to 30 people wanting to know what was going on. Ugandans are among the most kind, accepting and giving people I've met anywhere. Their struggle is that they just don't have the financial resources to help others as they would like. The average wage for a laborer is $35 a month. Individuals gave him what few coins they could, but it wasn't much to live on.

But now the onlookers began discussing Sekerena's plight. Together, they agreed he needed a job and a place to live. They started kicking around ideas. In front of them, they didn't see a disabled man or a foreigner or a refugee from another country. They just saw someone who needed a chance.

"If you could have a job, what would you like to do, considering your circumstances?" they asked him.

In the end, they decided that he could sell airtime minutes for cell phones. In Uganda, selling minutes for cell phones is a small business. You profit from selling the minutes themselves, but you also receive a bonus for recruiting others into the business.

Just then, a man wandering down the street joined the crowd and asked what was going on. It just so happened that he owned a cell phone franchise. Really, it was just a miracle—God's perfect timing!

This man was willing to mentor Sekerena, provide him with a job and with minutes to sell. He arranged it so that Sekerena would receive twice as much income as anybody else selling minutes, and he gave him free rein to sell his minutes in any territory he chose.

But the crowd wasn't finished yet.

"None of this is going to do him any good if he is homeless and he can't take care of himself," one man noted. "Come with me. I know of a place."

The crowd helped load Sekerena and his wheelchair into our truck and we took off. His new home was a room in a rowhouse-type of complex. It was about 100 square feet in all and had no windows, no electric, no running water and no bathroom. He'd have to use an outhouse that served about 100 people. But this is the norm for most people in Kampala.

Two of our service members provided three months' rent to get Sekerena started. After that, he would have to work hard to stay in the room, which cost almost as much as he could make in a month.

Sekerena had woken up that day a broken, homeless and hopeless man. He went to sleep that night with a whole new life. It all started with a simple vision, and the cooperation of some caring people. God provided the vision, and people just said, "Let us help."

Since leaving Uganda, I've heard from two people that Sekerena is working hard to sustain himself. Being a part of this incredible trans-formation has reaffirmed my faith that God has a plan for each of us. I have seen the power that is available when God moves and God's people say yes. In the end, we were all blessed by taking part in God's plan to give Sekerena a new life. We were blessed by saying yes.

Chaplain Richard "Mike" Warner is an Air Force chaplain. In his long military career, he has had many stateside assignments, as well as deployments to Iraq, Turkey, Korea, Japan and Djibouti. He is endorsed by the United Methodist Church and married to his high school sweetheart, Jo. They have two college-aged children, Sarah and David.

42

A BAPTISM AT SEA

CHAPLAIN JASON ROCHESTER

LIEUTENANT, U. S. NAVY (COAST GUARD)

While I was assigned to the USS *Essex* at the naval base at Sasebo, Japan, I came across a sailor fairly regularly who was indifferent to matters of faith. She wasn't involved in chapel activities at all. As a chief petty officer, she didn't go out of her way to refer anyone under her command to me when they had personal problems or needed guidance. She was respectful when our paths crossed, but not especially welcoming. She'd say hello, acknowledge my presence, but that's about it.

Over time, though, I began to notice a change in this sailor. She began attending chapel services, at first sporadically and then faithfully. *What is all this about?* I wondered.

Finally, she approached me and said she wanted to be baptized. That's when I heard her story.

This sailor had had her share of troubles in life. She had grown up unhappily in a tradition of harsh faith that was strict and judgmental. She had been married, but her marriage had ended in a hasty divorce. After the divorce, she felt unwelcome in the churches she had tried attending. Although she had at one time declared a personal faith, she was bitterly disappointed in God now.

But in her troubles, she had begun reading the Bible on her own. I believe that without faith, we cannot be at peace. In this sailor's case, I think her unhappiness prompted her to look for comfort and direction from God. And, in time, that's exactly what she found. She made a new profession of faith and began attending chapel services.

I was thrilled when she asked if she could be baptized. Logistically speaking, we had a big hurdle, though. Where do you find a baptistry aboard a ship?

The USS *Essex* is an amphibious assault ship with a flight deck large enough for helicopters and Harrier jets, which take off and land vertically. We would carry engines for these aircraft, which came in big fiberglass containers called engine cans. A half of the can looks something like a bathtub, hollowed out deeply in the center. For the baptism, we lined half an engine can with a tarp and filled it with water.

After the regular chapel service that Sunday, we all went up to the flight deck. It was a beautiful, sunny day in July. We were berthed at the pier in Cairns, Australia, with the waterway on one side of us, mountains in the background and the city spread out in front of us. About 20 of us gathered around as this sailor gave witness to her faith through the step of baptism.

When she came up out of the water—and the water was pretty cold, so we didn't linger!—she was so excited. She spoke of her gratitude for God's faithfulness in her life and his grace to her, even when she wasn't looking for it.

We didn't know then that God was continuing to extend his grace to her, even on that very day. Among the group of witnesses to the baptism that morning was one special sailor—a man who had recently become a believer and who would later become her husband. God does work in mysterious ways!

Chaplain Jason Rochester is a Navy chaplain currently serving at the Coast Guard station in Elizabeth City, North Carolina. He is an ordained Southern Baptist minister endorsed by the North American Mission Board. Before his military career, he was a pastor in Indiana, and in his five years of military service he has had three assignments, including his stint on board the USS Essex in Sasebo, Japan.

43

GOLFING IN A COMBAT ZONE

CHAPLAIN DAVID SIFFERD

MAJOR, U.S. ARMY RESERVE

Wherever you have golfers, they'll find a way to hit golf balls. Even in Iraq.

In 2006, I was deployed with the Psychological Operations Task Force to Camp Victory outside Baghdad. My office was in a trailer near the headquarters. It was littered with old sets of golf clubs. It looked like units before ours had been driving golf balls into a small lake on the base. I asked the first sergeant to get rid of all the paraphernalia. I kept just a few clubs, thinking maybe we'd be able to use them sometime. But we didn't have any golf balls. They were all in the lake, I guess.

I mentioned the golf clubs to my family, and pretty soon we got a few dozen balls from the college my daughter attended. As you can imagine, they were gone in an hour!

About this time, a friend of mine from high school, Adam Barr, asked me whether he could send me anything I wanted or needed. My wife Paula was taking good care of me—she had just sent me another shipment of white socks—so I asked Adam about sending me some used golf balls. It just so happens Adam works for The Golf Channel.

Well, Adam wrote a column asking readers and viewers to send over their used golf balls. I knew he had written it, but I just wasn't prepared for the outpouring! FedEx began dropping off boxes. Then, one day, they unloaded an entire crate of new balls—10,000 balls— from Top-Flite. After that, we began getting regular deliveries of golf clubs, hats, tees, golf socks, brush tees, rubber tees, ball pickers— anything and everything golf. Most came from individual golfers, golf communities and golfing clubs.

Before long, Wittek Golf Supply sent over some driving mats and rubber tees. I got the idea that instead of driving balls into the lake, I wanted to build a driving range. After making some inquiries, I got hooked up with someone at Camp Liberty who found us some wood and power tools.

I asked around: "Who'd like to help me build a driving platform?"

Well, of course, everyone wanted to help. What's not to like about power tools! Pretty soon, we had a 60-foot wooden deck and tee box covered with grass mats.

Behind my office was a large field, about 20 acres in size. The ground was rough and covered with tall brush. But it worked for us. We used old tires and pieces of wood as markers, and our driving range was up and running.

We couldn't just walk out into the field and pick up the balls, though. It was bordered by a 15-foot canal. You had to hit over the canal and into the field. Every few weeks, we'd take a Humvee out into the field and pick up the golf balls. It took a few hours, and it got pretty muddy in the winter, but everyone was happy to do it. It provided a little relief from the daily routine.

Pretty soon, we located some steel posts and put together a driving cage with some netting we had received. Although the driving range was no more dangerous than any other area, it was nice not to have to go out into the field so often. The field was surrounded by some palm trees and bushes, so we weren't completely visible. But you did draw small arms fire every so often.

By this time, we were getting so many golf clubs and golf balls I began packing up sets and bagging up balls for anyone who wanted them. The Morale and Welfare folks gave them away. Soldiers from other units began asking for them. Our driving range was getting quite a reputation.

One day, a guy from an ordnance unit showed up at my door. These are the people who clear IEDs off the road. Their job is dangerous and stressful, with little opportunity for relief, and it showed on the soldier's face. This fellow said he'd heard something about a driving range at Camp Victory. I took him out back and set him up. Within minutes, his whole demeanor changed. He began to relax and enjoy himself.

"This is just what I needed!" he exclaimed.

That's the way so many soldiers feel. For many who are deployed, it can get very tedious here, every day the same as the last for those who don't get outside the wire. For those who do, the stress of combat can build up. Every base has means of recreation—movies, computers, books, maybe a ping pong table or a pool table, in rare cases a volleyball court—but often there are very few opportunities to relieve stress physically. That's how I saw the driving range, as a way to relax and relieve the stress of combat and prepare for the jobs ahead.

We were grateful to everyone who sent us golf balls and golf equipment. We credit everything to the incredible support of the American people. We got golf balls from people coast to coast, thousands and thousands of balls. I sent e-mail thanks and a flag or a certificate of appreciation for every package we received. Almost every box of golf balls we got came with an encouraging note from the sender.

One note in particular touched my heart deeply. It was included in a box of balls we had received from an elderly woman in Chicago. The woman's husband had just recently died. He had been a golfer. The woman went out into her garage and retrieved boxes of her husband's used balls. She took them into the kitchen and carefully washed, dried and packed each one. The note included in the box was from the woman's daughter.

"My mother was thinking about my dad the whole time she prepared these golf balls for you," she wrote. "I know it was therapeutic for her. It was just what she needed right now."

For me, stories like this were the best part of the Camp Victory driving range.

Chaplain David Sifferd is a U.S. Army Reserve chaplain on active duty ordained and endorsed by the Church of the Nazarene. Before becoming a chaplain, he pastored churches in Maryland, Michigan and New York. Currently, he is assigned to the Army's 63rd Regional Support Command. He and his wife, Paula, have three children, Cirena, Deidra and David.

The Camp Victory driving range is still going strong. Later units bulldozed the field and cleared it of brush. On November 25, 2007, it was dedicated to the memory of Command Sgt. Maj. Jonathan Lankford, an avid golfer who died that year at Camp Victory. The dedication was attended by seven members of the Professional Golf Association—Tom Watson, David Feherty, Butch Harmon, Joe Inman, Tom Lehman, Frank Lickliter and Howard Twitty. The golfers spent three hours at the driving range, offering a clinic for the soldiers and touring the base.

"We, as golfers, are brothers," said Watson during the dedication ceremony. "It is an honor to be here and help dedicate this facility. My life is changed forever."

Watson went back to Camp Victory in November 2009. "I have tremendous admiration for our military," says Watson. "They are the very best people using an astounding breadth of sophisticated equipment to do the very best job possible." On his last visit, he did note, however, that the soldiers' golfing equipment has seen better days. "The artificial turf mats are looking pretty worn," he said. It may be time for a new round of donations.

44

IMMODERATE RAINS

CHAPLAIN JOSH WHITE
CAPTAIN, SOUTH CAROLINA ARMY NATIONAL GUARD

We have a saying in the Army: If it's not raining, you aren't training.

That's a joke of course, but it seems true more often than not. In training, soldiers have to prepare for 32 tasks, as well as 12 drills. In addition, they have to qualify on a variety of weapons. Rain slows everything down. The roads are nasty. It's hard to see when you shoot. Rain makes life generally miserable.

In the real world, of course, ideal conditions don't always exist either. But during training, it helps to have good weather, so that everyone learns what they need to know in order to stay alive.

My battalion is the 1/178 Field Artillery—the Swamp Fox Battalion, we're called, in honor of Brigadier General Francis Marion. We're an Army National Guard unit from South Carolina. I've served as chaplain here for two years. We are currently preparing for mobilization to Afghanistan.

Our first two weeks here it rained regularly, and when it wasn't raining it was overcast. Near the end of the second week, on a Thursday, the Master Gunner of our unit, a sergeant first class, asked me to step into his office. I was concerned that I had done something to interfere with training and that the sergeant was going to ask me—with the greatest respect, of course—to get out of the way. But that wasn't it at all.

"Chaplain," he said, "this weather is killing us. Could you please pray for some good weather so we can complete our training?"

I was speechless for a few seconds, but then answered in the affirmative. "Absolutely!" I said. "What dates would you like good weather?" I thought we might as well be specific! He gave me a list of dates.

Now, of course, the most famous weather prayer on record dates from World War II. Rain had plagued General Patton's Army throughout his campaigns in the fall of 1944, bogging down his troops as they tried to advance across Europe. On the morning of December 8, Patton placed a call at the Third Army Headquarters in Nancy, France, to the Chief Chaplain, Colonel James H. O'Neill.

"This is General Patton," he said to the chaplain. "Do you have a good prayer for weather? We must do something about those rains if we are to win the war."

Rifling through his prayer books, Father O'Neill couldn't find a prayer for good weather. So he composed his own.

Almighty and most merciful Father, we humbly beseech Thee, of Thy great goodness, to restrain these immoderate rains with which we have had to contend. Grant us fair weather for Battle. Graciously hearken to us as soldiers who call upon Thee that, armed with Thy power, we may advance from victory to victory, and crush the oppression and wickedness of our enemies and establish Thy justice among men and nations.

General Patton was pleased. "Chaplain," he said, "I am a strong believer in prayer. There are three ways that men get what they want—by planning, by working, and by praying." He had 250,000 copies of the prayer printed up and distributed to the entire Third Army. The bad weather continued, though, until December 20, when blue skies finally emerged over Bastogne. With the weather now perfect for flying, thousands of U.S. planes were able to knock out and drive back the German forces.

When General Patton next saw the chaplain, he said, "Well, Padre, our prayers worked. I knew they would." And he cracked Chaplain O'Neill on the side of his steel helmet with his riding crop.

This legendary story was on my mind when our Master Gunner asked me to pray about the weather. When I got back to my office, I wanted to go online and find that prayer to use as guidance. But my internet was down, so I sat down and prayed for a few minutes. I asked God what to write. It had been a while since I prayed with such boldness.

Then I began to type. I wrote in faith. I didn't know what the weather forecast was and I just believed that God would answer. When I finished, I had my chaplain's assistant read the prayer. His response was, "I think you should ask for good weather, but then include 'Your will be done.'" Now, of course, I always try to submit to God's will, but this time I believed that I needed to be bold and not hedge my bets, so to speak.

In part, here is what I wrote:

Almighty God, our Maker and Creator, we come to You with humble hearts. We know that we are completely unworthy of Your attention, and yet You pour out Your amazing love and grace upon us. . . . We thank You for the privilege of serving our country and the cause of freedom around the world. . . .

We ask now, Lord, for some clear weather. During this week, from 20–23 October, we need blue skies and cool temperatures in order to prepare for the task ahead to which You have called us. We know You have the power because You made the sun stand still in the sky for a whole day. We know You have the power because You calmed the storm with a word. We ask for that word now. . . .

We praise You for what You are going to do. We pray this in the Name that is above all Names, the name of Jesus. Amen!

I distributed my prayer to all the platoon leaders and asked them to pray the prayer with all of their soldiers who were willing. Many were glad to do this.

It is now Wednesday, October 21. As I work, I am looking out the window. I see blue skies and the temperature is cool. It is a gorgeous day. It has been this way for the last two days and it is forecast to be like this the rest of the week. Just yesterday, the Master Gunner came to me to thank me for my prayer. I told him that my prayer had no power in itself—it is the power of God that we are seeing at work.

But what is really exciting to me is that the results of my prayer aren't just about the weather. My credibility as a chaplain has skyrocketed! People are coming to me for prayer in greater numbers—prayer for themselves, prayer for their families, prayer for their marriages.

But it's not just others who have been touched by my weather prayer. I have been touched. I must admit, even as a chaplain, in recent years my faith had grown cold. I've been a Christian for 25 years, but I was like the church of Ephesus; I'd lost my first love. I talked about being passionately in love with Jesus, but I had lost my passion.

At one of my lowest points a few months ago, God spoke to me through Psalm 63: *O God, you are my God, earnestly I seek you; my soul thirsts for you, my body longs for you, in a dry and weary land where there is no water.*

I began praying this prayer for my life. Every day I would ask, "God, make me thirsty for You. Give me a desire for You. I want that passion!" God heard my prayer. He said to me, *Yes, I'm going to do this for you.* His words of encouragement spoke to my heart.

Seeing God work through the weather—in a wet and weary land where there was way too much water!—has been an answer to prayer. I don't deserve it. I am unworthy of this. Yet I cannot even begin to thank him enough for showing his power to me in such a direct way. I can't wait to continue to be used by him as we prepare to deploy.

Chaplain Josh White is battalion chaplain for the 1/178 Field Artillery, South Carolina Army National Guard. He is a Southern Baptist chaplain assigned through the North American Mission Board. Before joining the Army two years ago, he pastored in student and music ministries. He and his wife, Marilyn, have three children, Jesse, Ruthie and Mikey. In their family ministry, Engage, they sing and bring messages to church audiences.

45

PULL YOUR RESERVE!

CHAPLAIN ROBERT SAUNDERS

COLONEL, U.S. ARMY, RETIRED

After returning from Vietnam, I was assigned to the 101st Airborne Division at Fort Campbell, Kentucky. Before and after Vietnam, I trained to jump out of planes into combat zones, so I could go on field exercises with my soldiers.

One time at Fort Campbell, I was part of an evening training jump with the 326th Engineer Battalion, one of the units of the 101st Airborne. It would be dark by the time we hit the ground, but still daylight as we went through pre-jump activities and loaded the aircraft.

We flew for awhile until we were up about 1,200 feet. On this occasion, we were jumping simultaneously out of both sides of the aircraft. There were maybe 40 or 50 of us on the plane, and other planes in the air around us.

The order came to "Stand up, hook up!" So we did. When you jump out of a plane, you stand up and face the door. A light by the door turns green and then the jump master signals you to jump. All the others around you are yelling, "Go! Go! Go!" It gives you energy for the jump.

This time, though, evidently my exit was not as strong as it should have been. I may have paused for a millisecond at the door. I don't really know. But, quickly, I realized I was in trouble.

For some reason, I was falling faster than the jumpers around me. I glanced up at my parachute and saw the problem. One of the risers—the connecting cords running from my straps to the chute, that pull the chute out—had gotten caught over the top of the parachute. Instead of having one large canopy, I had two smaller canopies. That meant I had less air under the canopy. That's why I was falling faster than the others.

I was probably at about 800 feet and falling when I heard a voice close by me. It said, "Pull your reserve!"

God was speaking to me! In a flash, I imagined myself using this jump as a wonderful illustration of God's guiding voice wherever we are, even 800 feet up in the air. It would make a great sermon on Sunday—if I survived, that is.

Listening to the voice, I pulled out the reserve. A reserve chute is a pillow-shaped object on your chest. You pull the handle and it opens the container, and then you throw out the reserve.

But as I threw out the reserve, again I saw that something was wrong. Instead of deploying outward, the reserve went up into my main chute. This is another situation that reduces the amount of air under a canopy.

Somehow, the riser trapped over the chute had come loose and my main chute had fully deployed. That's why the reserve chute couldn't get beyond it.

Now I had to keep the reserve chute from getting twisted up with the main chute, or I'd be in even more trouble. I pulled my reserve back in as best I could, holding it tightly to my chest.

I completed the jump with my main parachute working as it should have been. I landed in the best way I knew how, feet together, on the balls of my feet and going into a roll to prevent injury as much as possible.

As I came in, the riggers, the people who pack your parachutes, ran out to meet me, along with various other authorities on the drop zone. They surrounded me on the ground, checking me over for damage. Pretty quickly, they determined that all my bones were intact.

Just then, an Airborne Engineer Lieutenant emerged from the crowd. Coming along beside me, he whispered into my ear.

"Did you hear me?" he asked. "I jumped the other door as you were jumping your door, and I saw that you were in trouble. I spread my arms and legs out to get over to you, and I shouted, 'Pull your reserve!'"

Can the Lord speak in a Midwestern accent through an Airborne Engineer Lieutenant? Well, I can assure you, He did! The Lord can speak to you in any situation, even when you're jumping out of an aircraft. And that's something to preach about!

Chaplain Robert Saunders retired as a U.S. Army chaplain in 1986. He joined the Army in 1957 as a Reservist and went on active duty in 1961. In addition to his domestic postings, he was deployed to Panama, Germany, Korea and Vietnam. Ordained a Southern Baptist minister, and later an American Baptist, he has served in retirement as a hospice chaplain and director of a rescue mission, among other ministries. He and his wife, Chaplain Lorraine Potter, a retired U.S. Air Force Major General, live in San Antonio, Texas.

46

WHERE'S OUR ICE CREAM?

CHAPLAIN GLYGER BEACH

COLONEL, U.S. ARMY RESERVE, RETIRED

Morale in the military has a lot to do with food. We're American! Give us a cheeseburger! That's what keeps our spirits up.

When I was stationed in Balad, Iraq, we had a McDonald's, we had a Pizza Hut. I drank a lot of Green Beans coffee! I was the garrison chaplain for the 301st Support Group. Part of my job was to report on morale.

One day, while I was eating at the DFAC, some soldiers came up to me and wanted to know what happened to the ice cream. We always enjoyed a lot of ice cream, a lot of different flavors. But there hadn't been any for weeks.

"We want our ice cream! Where's our ice cream?" they wanted to know. I told them I'd find out.

What you might not realize is that a lot of civilians work for private companies as truck drivers for the military. That's how we get all our supplies. They live on the base and are sometimes retired military, but very often they are younger people, both men and women, with spouses and children back home.

When I arrived at the base in 2004, some of these truck drivers sought me out to ask me to find a place where they could worship and have Bible studies. I found them a place in a large building a private contractor was constructing on the base. Some of them were ordained as ministers in the States and they conducted their own services, but sometimes they asked me to speak, and I began to counsel them as I did our military members. They were very appreciative.

At the soldiers' request, I went to my truck drivers to ask them about the ice cream. I soon learned the reason we hadn't had any.

"The ice cream truck was blown up by an IED," the truckers told me. "The driver of the truck died."

The news brought me up short. Here we were demanding our ice cream, and we didn't know that an American civilian had died bringing it to us.

I learned that day that many truck drivers are killed in service to their country. Many times, they don't even get a memorial service, because nobody knows they've died. Nobody hears it on the evening news. Nobody knows they're here. They feel totally isolated.

That day, I listened to the drivers' stories of courage and commitment, and of their sacrifices. I prayed with them and I cried with them, and I developed a deep appreciation for their service to our country. Before my deployment ended, I conducted a memorial service for four truckers who had died on the road. Each one had a family back home; the oldest was just 42 years old. I made sure everybody on the base knew about the service. The room that day was filled to overflowing.

I thank God for these unsung American heroes who risk their lives for the country they love.

Chaplain Glyger Beach is a retired U.S. Army Reserve chaplain. Born in St. Vincent and the Grenadines, he came to the United States in 1972 and served for 27 years in the Reserves. He is a United Methodist pastor in Brooklyn, New York. He and his wife, Candace, have six children; Andrew, Leticia, Ashley, Stephen, Christian and Justin.

47

LAYING DOWN OUR SORROWS

CHAPLAIN JAMES PENNINGTON

CAPTAIN, U.S. ARMY

Weeping may remain for a night,

but rejoicing comes in the morning.

PSALM 30:5

One thing that I will always associate with my deployment to Iraq in 2004 is the worship song "Trading My Sorrows." I first heard it while attending the chapel at Forward Operating Base Marez. We sang it at almost every service, because the words expressed so exactly what we were all feeling. There, in a war zone, we sang of laying down our sorrow, our sickness, our pain and opening our hearts to the joy that only the Lord can give.

The song was usually our closing song. After we had finished, as a benediction, I would say, "Go and live for Jesus and whatever He tells you to do, you say, 'Yes Lord'." My words echoed the chorus that followed each verse of the song.

One night after a Bible study, I noticed one of our staff sergeants hanging back. He was one of our best non-commissioned officers—Airborne, Air Assault qualified and at one time a recruiter. After this deployment, he would go on to volunteer with an elite Ranger Battalion, and he was deployed again four months later.

This soldier was a very faithful chapel member. Often, he would arrive early or come late, or he would have to leave in the middle of chapel, depending on his missions. So, I sensed that this time he was staying around after the study for some reason. After everyone else had left, I approached him and asked if anything was wrong.

He told me that on his last convoy his vehicle had been struck by an IED. He and his crew were all okay, but he was visibly shaken, trembling with emotion. I reached out for his hand to give him a handshake. Then, I pulled him forward and gave him a quick hug and said, "Let's pray."

"I'd like to pray," he said. "But I'd like to pray up front."

In the front of the chapel was a platform. On it stood a six-foot wooden cross. The cross had been a gift to the chapel from a few of our members.

There in front of the cross, the staff sergeant knelt down and bowed his head. He placed a hand on the cross. I stood beside him and put my hand on his shoulder. He uttered a quiet, emotion-laden prayer. I couldn't hear all of the words, but I felt the power of his prayer. Through it all, I prayed silently for him. After a few moments in prayer, he stopped trembling and he fell silent. He stood up and looked me in the eye.

"I'm good now, Chaplain," he said. "I've got to go. I have soldiers to take care of."

With that, he turned and walked from the chapel. After he left, I stayed and soaked up that holy moment. I thought about how at the foot of the cross, this soldier had laid down his sorrows. Through the cross, God takes our pain from us and, in its place, he gives us his peace and joy.

Chaplain James Pennington is an Army chaplain endorsed by the North American Mission Board of the Southern Baptist Church. He has served for 18 years in the military, as an active enlisted soldier, enlisted National Guardsman and in the Army Reserve. He has been an active duty chaplain since 2004, and was deployed to Iraq in 2004–05. Prior to his military service, he worked in industrial sales and as an associate pastor in Tennessee and Mississippi. He and his wife, Jenny, have two sons, Luke and Nicholas.

48

I'M DOING FINE

CHAPLAIN BARRY WHITE

LIEUTENANT COLONEL, U.S. ARMY, RETIRED

I have learned to be content whatever the circumstances.

PHILIPPIANS 4:11

As I boarded the military transport plane, I looked around and saw wounded soldiers everywhere. Those who were ambulatory sat around the outsides of the cabin. The more seriously injured lay in litters on racks in the center, three litters to a rack.

This is part of my job, to meet the planes coming into Andrews Air Force Base from Germany carrying our wounded soldiers from Afghanistan and Iraq. From this plane, the ones who are less seriously wounded are taken to the hospital at Andrews. The next morning, they are flown to hospitals near their assigned bases. Those who are in worse condition are transported to Walter Reed Army Medical Center or the U.S. Naval Medical Center in Bethesda for treatment.

When I meet these flights, I board the plane and make my way around from soldier to soldier, talking with one, praying with another. On this particular flight, in July 2009, I began with the less seriously wounded soldiers around the perimeter. Out of the corner of my eye, I saw the medical crew prepping the most critically wounded soldier in the plane, a lieutenant colonel who had lost both of his legs to an IED and was suffering from massive internal injuries.

Finally, after the wounded officer had been tended to, I came around to his litter. I bent down so I could look him in the eyes and hear him if he spoke. Leaning in, I began to tell him who I was. He couldn't talk very well, but he didn't let me get very far before he broke in.

"Chaplain," he said, "I'm doing fine."

He looked up at me as he continued.

"The Holy Spirit is with me and I'm doing okay," he said. "You don't have to worry about me."

The officer's look of confidence reflected a wondrous peace in his heart.

I was taken totally off guard. Just when I thought I was the one bringing comfort and support, this grievously wounded officer gave me that and more. In his situation, I could have understood despair, or anger, or bitterness, or at best indifference. His circumstance was one that would test anyone's faith. Yet he was sure without a doubt that God was looking after him. What an awesome moment! What an awesome faith.

Chaplain Colonel Barry White retired after a 22-year career in the U.S. Army as a United Methodist chaplain. For a brief time before entering the military, he was a pastor at three churches in North Carolina and Florida. He has served deployments to Hawaii and Guantanamo Bay. He and his wife, Lisa, have two sons, Matthew and Mark, and one grandson, Landon.

49

ON THE MAINE LINE

CHAPLAIN SHERI SNIVELY

COMMANDER, U.S. NAVY RESERVE

On an early morning, only two days into the month of February, I looked out the window of the plane at the Maine coastline covered in snow and ice. The scene warmed me. There were hills and trees. Two-story houses formed a dot-to-dot pattern across the landscape. Smoke rose from the chimneys of the homes and the stacks of local industry. Each curling plume gave evidence that someone was awake this early winter morning.

Would they be there for us today? I wondered. It was awfully early on a cold February morning, so I didn't want to get my hopes up too high only to be disappointed.

The plane landed, and we walked corridor after winding corridor as we made our way from Gate 6. Finally, we rounded the last corner and the passageway opened into the international airport terminal at Bangor. In the distance, down the long sloping hallway, I could see shops sparkling with lights and goodies for sale: gift shops, a bookstore, a coffeehouse.

But then the best sight of all came into view.

There he was: an old gray-haired man, bent and leaning on a cane, standing midway down the passageway, front and center such that no one got by him without shaking his hand. My heart soared.

I had heard about the Maine Troop Greeters. Veterans have been at Bangor International Airport every day since Operation Desert Storm, greeting troops as they depart for and return from Iraq and Afghanistan. They offer kind words, muffins, cookies, free cell phone calls.

I smiled, my eyes welling with tears. There he stood, as tall and proud as his 80-odd years would allow. "Welcome home. Job well done," he said to me. He said it with warmth and enthusiasm as each of us passed by his post.

His World War II baseball cap told his story—you've seen the kind, with the WWII-era ribbons embroidered on the front and "WWII Veteran" lettered neatly above and below. He'd been there. Exactly where, who knows? Which branch, who knows? None of that matters now. What matters is the warm embrace of one who knows.

I wondered whether he was the lone greeter that morning. But then I saw the others forming a gauntlet. They were there! The Maine Troop Greeters were there! The people of Maine were here to greet us and welcome us home. I was so excited. I felt just like a 5-year-old on Christmas morning.

These were men and women who had served in World War II, Korea, or Vietnam; each had his own war, each his own experience. There were battles on the sea and in the air, on the ground in the jungles and in other far-flung places seemingly godforsaken then and now largely forgotten by everyone except those who served there. Names like Guadalcanal, Puson, Inchon, or Da Nang mean something deeply personal

to them, the same way the names of places like Fallujah, Ramadi, Hab-
baniyah or Al Taqqadum now hold meaning for me. The names and
places are different, even the experiences themselves in ways are very
different, yet warrior to warrior, there is a bond that transcends time.

Just a few days earlier, I had watched at the Al Taqqadam morgue
as my Marines processed the remains of four Army soldiers who
wouldn't be receiving a hug from the old World War II veteran standing in the passageway in Maine. Yes, they were home now. They, too,
had received a homecoming welcome—just not the kind they had
hoped for. There was no warm embrace for them. Instead, loved ones
probably wept and embraced one another. No, the four Army guys
couldn't feel the warmth of a physical embrace anymore. They were
embraced now instead by the icy arms of death.

After the short refueling and pit stop, we loaded back onto the
plane. I returned to my window seat near the front. I sat alone in the
row. The serene early winter morning was haunting in its beauty.
It was peaceful and comforting but also lonely and desolate, even
depressing. My eyes welled with tears. Those Army soldiers should
have been coming home in a few months to shake hands with the old
Army guys that stand duty here. But they never will. I let the tears
flow unabated down my cheeks.

*Chaplain Sheri Snively is a Quaker chaplain in the U.S. Navy Reserve. She
deployed to Iraq with the First Marine Logistics Group from Camp Pendle-
ton, California. She is the mother of two sons, Andrew and Matthew. "On
the Maine Line" is excerpted and adapted with permission from Chaplain
Snively's book,* Heaven in the Midst of Hell *(Raven Oaks Press, 2010).*

50

THE PRESENCE OF CHRIST IN A WAR ZONE

CHAPLAIN GORDON TERPSTRA

LIEUTENANT COLONEL,

U.S. ARMY RESERVE, RETIRED

As I lie awake each night in Iraq, I ache with homesickness for the abundant water, the evergreen trees, the peaceable mountains, the lush farmlands, and the loving safety of my home in Washington State. This is the most difficult year of my life and yet, paradoxically, the most deepening and meaningful. I would not relive this year, but neither would I trade it. Go figure.

The tests here are arduous, and they stretch my soul. But the growth of spirit and the meaningfulness of ministry are every bit as tangible as the ordeals. It is a year of terrible trial yet beautiful blessing . . . a paradox for this Army chaplain.

My assignment is Phoenix Base in Baghdad, where I am responsible for 900 soldiers. I also fly across the country to distant FOBs (Forward Operating Bases), where I minister to another 300 scattered soldiers. Mostly I travel via Blackhawk helicopter, but occasionally we convoy into the Red Zone. I never sleep well the night before we fly over dangerous areas.

As chaplain to these troops, I counsel them, befriend them, conduct their chapel services, listen to their heartaches, sit with them in their tears, pray for them when they are wounded, and hug them when they need it. I conduct their memorial services if they die. I perform these ministries no matter what their faith or lack of faith. An Army chaplain serves every soldier in the unit.

The Worst Day

What a trial this war is! The most graphic cost has been performing six memorial services for seven of our soldiers. One was for a 24-year-old airman who only had two weeks of service left before he could return to his wife and little girls.

In March 2008, a rocket attack killed two and wounded 18. That attack knocked me to the ground. I spent all afternoon and evening in the hospital, praying with the wounded, crying with the grieving, and committing the deceased into the gracious arms of the Lord. The floor was awash in blood. At day's end I dropped my body armor onto the floor of my hutch with a thud and literally collapsed into bed. The next day I began counseling those with survivor's guilt and ongoing trauma.

Colonel Stephen Scott was one of our two KIAs (Killed in Action) that horrific day. A few weeks before, he had approached me in the mess hall with a sunny smile and thanked me for the message about heaven I'd given that morning in chapel. Now, as I stared into his lifeless face, contorted in violent death, I wondered what it was like for him to be with Jesus his Savior.

Another killed that day was Major Stu Wolfer. I sat between two Army captains with my arms around their shoulders as they wept over their dear friend. Sometimes ministry is simply being present as people weep—even tough Army captains need to cry. That very night I gazed down at those two black body bags ready to be airlifted out to the States. We call these "Angel Flights." Indeed, may God's angels bear them home. We all stood saluting in the dark until the choppers were gone.

That horrible day in the hospital was its own paradox. On the one hand I felt so helpless. I am not a doctor or a nurse. All I could do was walk among the wounded, touch them, say a prayer, be present, hold those who wept, and pray over the dead. I could not do anything medical for them. I felt so inept.

On the other hand, in that very weakness was God's power. To be present in the name of the Lord, to pray, to touch as Jesus would touch, to read Psalm 23, and to weep with those who weep is to feel divine strength.

Ongoing Trials

Trials continue. Seventeen soldiers came to me after their spouses in the States told them their marriages were over. Sit with me and listen to their agony. Or stand with me by the bed of a 24-year-old soldier whose right leg was just amputated because of a bomb attack. Or listen with me to a high-ranking officer as he expresses his raw fear. Or sit with a suicidal soldier and try to bring some sanity back into his life.

We have endured more than 460 rocket attacks this year. Continual dashes to bunkers become a daily habit. After one attack I held a sergeant in my arms as he sobbed on my chest, realizing how close he came to never seeing his little boy again.

We often awaken at 6:00 a.m. to the warning siren as another attack comes in. At those times, all I can do is lie there and pray, with my heart racing and sweat pouring off my forehead. The crack of a rocket hitting 50 feet away punches home how quickly life can be over.

I also minister to the Iraqi workers on base. One morning I arrived at Phoenix Base to discover that one of our translators had been found beheaded in the Tigris River. We gathered in a room for prayer and to calm the other workers' terror-stricken hearts.

I walk to our church service on Sunday morning as the sound of a gun battle resounds a few blocks away. You get used to it. Or you hear the explosion and feel the concussion of a suicide truck bomber trying to crash our gate, and you wonder how many people died in that instant. You get used to that too. You hear the MedEvac helicopters ferrying the wounded and dying to the hospital all day and all night. I will never forget that day-in, day-out drone.

You trudge into your empty hutch night after night without your loving spouse to greet you, thinking, "How many nights can I endure this, Lord?"

Ongoing Blessings

Paradoxically, blessing and meaning live here as well.

Chapel services on Sunday run 120 soldiers. They don't care about the worship wars of churches back home. They just want to sit in the presence of God and be fed in their souls. They crave assurance that God is with them in this place.

And there is the blessing of being present for a soldier who needs a human pastor to sit with him as he cries. Or the blessing of wearing the cross on my uniform where soldiers can see it and be reminded that God is here. Or the beauty of how God uses this desert experience to enlarge my soul and deepen my walk with him. Or the openness of 500 soldiers at Staff Sergeant Chris Frost's memorial service to the statement before the message: "In a time of sadness like this, we need to hear a word from the Lord." Or the blessing of praying for our troops and their families with my chaplain assistant, Staff Sergeant John Lucero, as we arrive at Phoenix Base each morning.

All this is part of what your military chaplains continue to do each day in Iraq and Afghanistan, in places where the touch of Christ is especially needed. That is why we wear the cross on our uniform—not to endorse war, but to be the living presence of the Prince of Peace in these places too. Yes, even here.

Chaplain Gordon Terpstra was a Christian Reformed Church chaplain with the U.S. Army Reserve for 20 years. He served in the Marine Corps as an enlisted soldier during the Vietnam War, pastored four churches and served twice on active duty, first during Desert Storm and then in 2007–08 in Iraq. Currently he is a hospice chaplain. He and his wife, Cheryl, have four children, Timothy, Kevin, Troy and Sara.

Acknowledgements

My moment of grace came in September 2009 when Gary and Rosalind Ziccardi sat down at our dinner table and told me a story. My eureka moment—military chaplains have wonderful stories to tell!—is all due to these two friends. Thank you, Gary and Rosalind.

Because of my agent, Bill Jensen, I was ready to go the very next day. He had this book on the shelves before I wrote even one word of it. Bill, I am still celebrating.

It has been a joy to work with Leafwood Publishers. Leonard Allen and Gary Myers had a vision for this book, and Heidi Nobles got me off to a great start. All of Leafwood's fine people made it happen. Their confidence in me and in this book kept me going.

Many people helped me find my way around military circles, among them Chaplain Beverly Barnett, a friend of my parents who took me under his wing; Chaplain Major General Cecil R. Richardson, Chief of Chaplains, USAF; Chaplain Colonel Edward T. Brogan, USAF, Retired, director of the Presbyterian Council for Chaplains and Military Personnel; and Chaplain Brigadier General Douglas E. Lee, U.S. Army, Retired, executive director of the Presbyterian & Reformed Joint Commission on Chaplains and Military Personnel. Numerous endorsing agencies sent out requests for stories, while military support agencies such as CatholicMil.org and Strength for Service did the same. Newspaper editors and reporters generously shared their sources with me.

Lastly, I'm breezing through life with my own personal patron of the arts, my husband John, whose love and support makes my writing life possible. My son Evan brings love and laughter to my days, which gives depth to my writing. Their contribution to this book is the real story.

ENDNOTES

Introduction

1. Parker C. Thompson, *From Its European Antecedents to 1791: The United States Army Chaplaincy* (Washington, D.C.: Department of the Army, Office of the Chief of Chaplains, 1978), pp. 106–07.

2. Joel Tyler Headley, *The Chaplains and Clergy of the American Revolution* (New York: Charles Scribner, 1864; reprint, Collingswood, N.J.: Christian Beacon, 1976), p. 85.

3. Headley, p. 85

4. Thompson, pp. 195–96.

5. Dan Kurzman, *No Greater Glory: The Four Immortal Chaplains and the Sinking of the Dorchester in World War II* (New York: Random House Trade Paperback, 2005), p. 144.

6. The Four Chaplains Memorial Foundation (www.fourchaplains.org).

7. Daniel Poling, *Mine Eyes Have Seen* (New York: McGraw Hill, 1959), p. 204.

INDEX

Alphabetical List of Chaplains and Others

Aleson, Dennis (Lieutenant Colonel, USAF, Ret.), 191

Alexander, David (Lieutenant, USN, Marines), 134

Barnett, Beverly (Lieutenant Colonel, USAF, Ret.), 122

Barnett, Eddie (Lieutenant Colonel, USA), 92

Barr, Adam (The Golf Channel), 204–05

Baugham, Billy (Major, USA, Ret.), 82

Bazer, Laurence (Lieutenant Colonel, ARNG), 102

Beach, Glyger (Colonel, USAR, Ret.), 217

Bean, Walter (Lieutenant Colonel, USAF), 61

Bellamy, Chad (Captain, USAF), 87

Blount, James (Major, USA), 20

Bohr, Timothy (Major, USAR), 77

Carlson, Harold (Colonel, USA, Ret.), 170

Garcia, Wayne (Major, USA), 154

Giles, Stan (Lieutenant Colonel, USANG), 108

Gills, Thomas (Major, USAF), 36

Groth, John (Lieutenant Colonel, USAFR, Ret.), 113

Hazlett, Gregg (Lieutenant, USN), 65

Hesseling, Jason (Major, USA), 147

Hoffman, Brad (Commander, USNR), 102

Hunt, Henry Lamar (Colonel, USA, Ret.), 48

Johnson, Dudley (Commander, USN, Ret.), 143

Lawhorn, Joseph (Captain, USA), 95

Lewis, Brad (Captain, USA), 140

Little, Dallas (Captain, USAF), 126

Logan, William "Dave" (Captain, USAF), 176

Mariya, Deborah Luethje (Lieutenant Commander, USN, Ret.), 151

Martin, Richard (Colonel, USA, Ret.), 130

Martindale, Joanne (Lieutenant Colonel, ARNG), 30

Morris, John (Major, ARNG), 159

Owen, John (Commander, USN), 117

Pennington, James (Captain, USA), 220

Peters, Jason (Major, USAF), 163

Potter, Lorraine (Major General, USAF, Ret.), 99

Pucciarelli, George (Captain, USN, Ret.), 52

Reeder, Christopher (Captain, USAF), 68

Resnicoff, Arnold (Captain, USN, Ret.), 52

Rochester, Jason (Lieutenant, USN, Coast Guard), 201

Rojas, Richard (Captain, USAF), 179

Routzahn, John (Lieutenant Colonel, USA), 95

Satterfield, Steven (Captain, USA), 43

Saunders, Robert (Colonel, USA, Ret.), 214

Schaick, Steven (Colonel, USAF), 73

Schrum, Ev (Colonel, USAF, Ret.), 167

Seo, William (Corporal, USA, Medic), 43

Sherer, Barbara (Colonel, USA), 173

Sifferd, David (Major, USAR), 204

Sinise, Gary (actor), 43–47

Snively, Sheri (Commander, USNR), 225

Stanley, Jack (Major, USAF), 186

Terpstra, Gordon (Lieutenant Colonel, USAR, Ret.), 228

Waite, Captain Douglas (Captain, USN), 27

Warner, Richard "Mike" (Lieutenant Colonel, USAF), 196

Watson, Tom (PGA golfer), 208

Weber, Chuck (Major, USA, Flight Surgeon), 185

Wheeler, Danny (Commander, USNR), 52

White, Barry (Lieutenant Colonel, USA, Ret.), 223

White, Josh (Captain, ARNG), 209

White, Michael (Major, USA), 39

Ziccardi, Gary (Lieutenant Colonel, USAF), 11–14

Chaplains by Branch of Service

Air Force

Aleson, Dennis (Lieutenant Colonel, Ret.), 191

Barnett, Beverly (Lieutenant Colonel, Ret.), 122

Bean, Walter (Lieutenant Colonel), 61

Bellamy, Chad (Captain), 87

Gills, Thomas (Major), 36

Little, Dallas (Captain), 126

Logan, William "Dave" (Captain), 176
Peters, Jason (Major), 163
Potter, Lorraine (Major General, Ret.), 99
Reeder, Christopher (Captain), 68
Rojas, Richard (Captain), 179
Schaick, Steven (Colonel), 73
Schrum, Ev (Colonel, Ret.), 167
Stanley, Jack (Major), 186
Warner, Richard "Mike" (Lieutenant Colonel), 196
Ziccardi, Gary (Lieutenant Colonel), 11–14

Air Force Reserve
Groth, John (Lieutenant Colonel, Ret.), 113

Air National Guard
Giles, Stan (Lieutenant Colonel, Tennessee), 108

Army
Barnett, Eddie (Lieutenant Colonel), 92
Baugham, Billy (Major, Ret.), 82
Blount, James (Major), 20
Carlson, Harold (Colonel, Ret.), 170
Garcia, Wayne (Major), 154
Hesseling, Jason (Major), 147
Hunt, Henry Lamar (Colonel, Ret.), 48
Lawhorn, Joseph (Captain), 95
Lewis, Brad (Captain), 140
Martin, Richard (Colonel, Ret.), 130
Pennington, James (Captain), 220
Routzahn, John (Lieutenant Colonel), 95
Saunders, Robert (Colonel, Ret.), 214
Sherer, Barbara (Colonel), 173
White, Barry (Lieutenant Colonel, Ret.), 223

Army Reserve
Beach, Glyger (Colonel, Ret.), 217
Bohr, Timothy (Major), 77
Sifferd, David (Major), 204
Terpstra, Gordon (Lieutenant Colonel, Ret.), 228

Army National Guard

Bazer, Laurence (Lieutenant Colonel, Massachusetts), 102
Martindale, Joanne (Lieutenant Colonel, New Jersey), 30
Morris, John (Major, Minnesota), 159
Satterfield, Steven (Captain, Colorado), 43
White, Josh (Captain, South Carolina), 209
White, Michael (Major, Alabama), 39

Navy

Alexander, David (Lieutenant, Marine Corps), 134
Hazlett, Gregg (Lieutenant), 65
Johnson, Dudley (Commander, Ret.), 143
Mariya, Deborah Luethje (Lieutenant Commander, Ret.), 151
Owen, John (Commander), 117
Pucciarelli, George (Captain, Ret.), 52
Resnicoff, Arnold (Captain, Ret.), 52
Rochester, Jason (Lieutenant, Coast Guard), 201
Waite, Douglas (Captain), 27

Navy Reserve

Hoffman, Brad (Commander), 102
Snively, Sheri (Commander), 225
Wheeler, Danny (Commander), 52

About the Author

Nancy B. Kennedy worked as a journalist for many years, including a stint as an editor for Dow Jones's pioneering electronic news service. As a financial writer, she worked for many newspapers and magazines, including the *New York Times* and the online *Wall Street Journal*, and for the financial services firm Merrill Lynch.

Ms. Kennedy has authored two children's books, both teacher resources that combine science activities with stories of the Christian faith—*Even the Sound Waves Obey Him* (Concordia, 2005) and *Make It, Shake It, Mix It Up* (Concordia, 2008). She continues to write articles and personal essays for books, magazines and newspapers. Many can be found at her website, www.nancybkennedy.com.

Ms. Kennedy lives in Hopewell, New Jersey, with her husband John, and their son, Evan.